TALLAHASSEE

Tradition, Technology & Teamwork

TALLAHASSEE

Tradition, Technology & Teamwork

Written By
Julie S. Bettinger & Heidi Tyline King
Corporate Profiles By
Andi Milam Reynolds

◆

Featuring the Photography of
Robert M. Overton

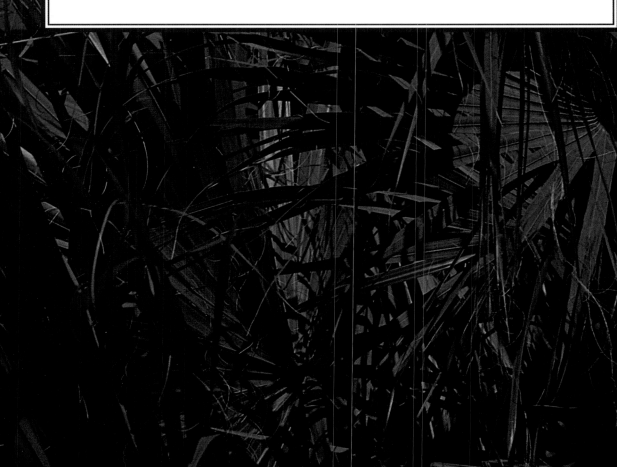

TABLE OF CONTENTS

TALLAHASSEE'S ENTERPRISES

FOREWORD

The Tallahassee Area Chamber of Commerce and its board of directors is pleased to present *Tallahassee: Tradition, Technology, and Teamwork.* In our estimation, this beautiful book dramatizes the rich heritage and bright promise of one of America's most distinctive communities and the people who make it so.

Tallahassee and Leon County are steeped in tradition dating not only to the earliest European exploration of the "New World" but also into the fathomless reaches of time when pre-Colombian peoples dwelled in this region of ideal climate and abundant natural resources.

The time line continues through the Christmastime visit of the explorer de Soto, the founding of the San Luis Spanish mission, and Tallahassee's establishment as Florida's capital in 1845. It continues with the emergence of great colleges and universities, neighborhoods in forested settings that draw people from across the nation, and internationally acclaimed research facilities only moments down the road from ancient Indian mounds on the shores of Lake Jackson.

However, this is not a history book. Tallahassee's past is already well documented. Instead, this publication looks to the future. In the words of the Tallahasseeans who wrote and illustrated it, the book is an expression of pride felt by people who live and work here and have teamed together to build a bright tomorrow. It serves, as well, as an invitation to others who we hope will come and share our bounty with us.

Sincere thanks to all who made this book possible. Your contribution will be appreciated for years to come.

◆

—James R. Ashlock
President
Tallahassee Area Chamber of Commerce

To tell the Tallahassee story . . . for a native Tallahasseean who had tasted the fruits of other communities before returning to this land we call "God's country"— it was the dream assignment. I can't help it— I love this place.

Even more important, I'm proud to be a part of a community of people who continue to work to preserve and enhance the area's assets for future generations. I plan to be part of that future, writing about people's lives, businesses, experiences, and savoring every moment I'm given on this green earth.

Writing a book such as this is a collaborative effort. I appreciate the fabulous working relationships I enjoyed with two of Tallahassee's more talented writers: Andi Reynolds and Heidi Tyline King.

I appreciate the faith that continues to be a well-spring of inspiration for my writing. I couldn't do it, of course, without my husband—Jim Bettinger—who provides a solid foundation for my work and my life. I would also like to extend great thanks and gratitude to my parents, Buddy and June Strauss, and family, including my loving in-laws, Cliff and Eleanor Bettinger.

Thank you, too, to the editors who give me opportunities to grow personally and professionally, and my clients and reading audience who help keep us all in business.

The contributors to this book are too numerous to mention—but you know who you are and I thank you with all my heart.

—Julie S. Bettinger

◆

I grew up in the country—Haleyville, Alabama, to be exact, so I know what it's like to run through pastures sprinkled with black-eyed Susans, to share two-lane roads with tractors, to sit down to a supper of home-grown corn and beans snapped that very afternoon.

Yet I've also experienced the city life of Birmingham, where quaint restaurants with fabulous food welcome you at every corner, where the number of shopping malls can't be counted on one hand, where an evening of entertainment lies just outside your door.

Moving to Tallahassee gave me a little bit of both places dearest to my heart. It's large enough to have choices, small enough to still be neighborly. Some nights, Creed and I will sit on the back porch, watching deer graze under the oak canopies and listening to the throaty tunes of croaking bullfrogs. On the other evenings, we'll meet friends for a night on the town, usually stopping first at our favorite restaurant before heading to a concert or hockey game. Yes, I'd have to say that here, in Tallahassee, lies the best of both worlds.

Thank you to Creed, who really listens, to the numerous Tallahasseeans who assisted me during my research, and to all our friends who have made Tallahassee feel like home.

—Heidi Tyline King

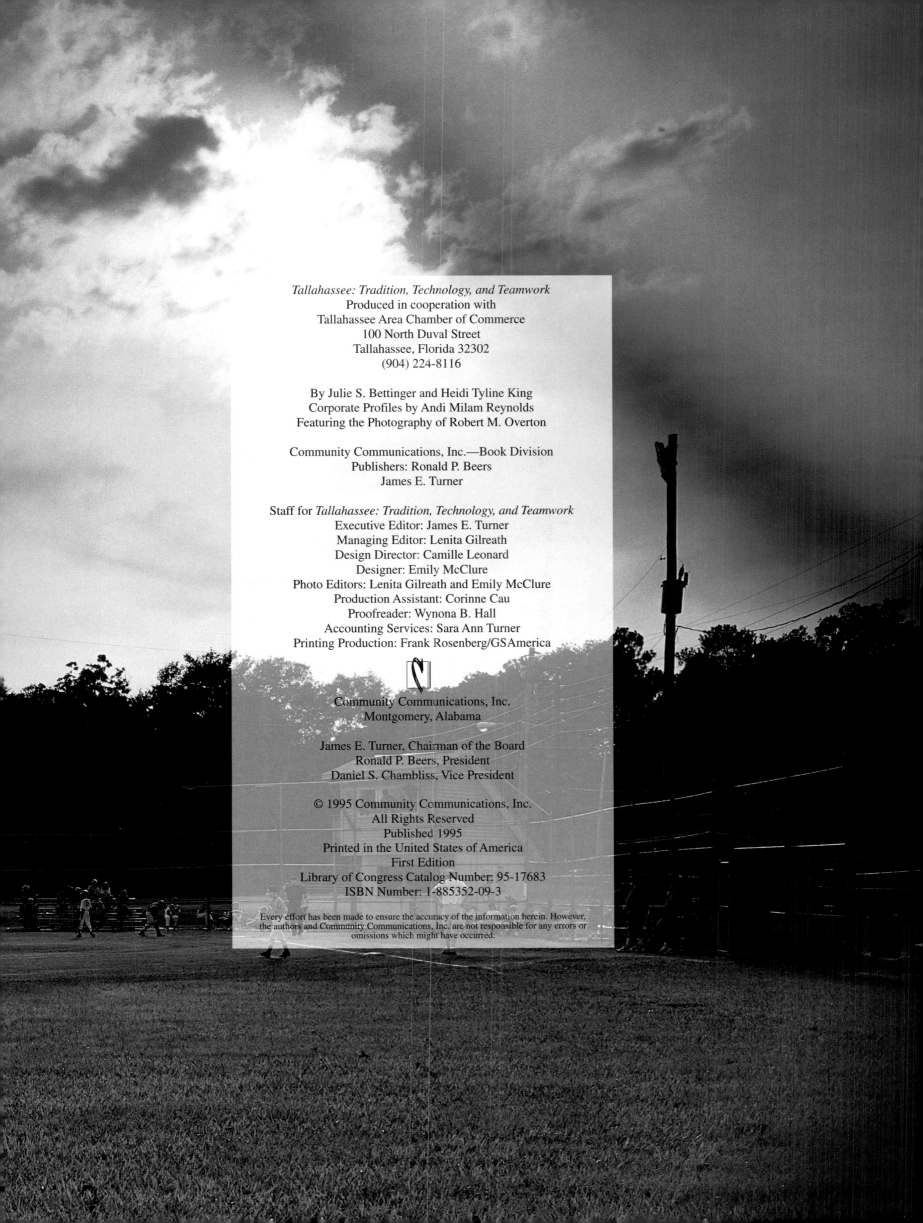

Tallahassee: Tradition, Technology, and Teamwork
Produced in cooperation with
Tallahassee Area Chamber of Commerce
100 North Duval Street
Tallahassee, Florida 32302
(904) 224-8116

By Julie S. Bettinger and Heidi Tyline King
Corporate Profiles by Andi Milam Reynolds
Featuring the Photography of Robert M. Overton

Community Communications, Inc.—Book Division
Publishers: Ronald P. Beers
James E. Turner

Staff for *Tallahassee: Tradition, Technology, and Teamwork*
Executive Editor: James E. Turner
Managing Editor: Lenita Gilreath
Design Director: Camille Leonard
Designer: Emily McClure
Photo Editors: Lenita Gilreath and Emily McClure
Production Assistant: Corinne Cau
Proofreader: Wynona B. Hall
Accounting Services: Sara Ann Turner
Printing Production: Frank Rosenberg/GSAmerica

Community Communications, Inc.
Montgomery, Alabama

James E. Turner, Chairman of the Board
Ronald P. Beers, President
Daniel S. Chambliss, Vice President

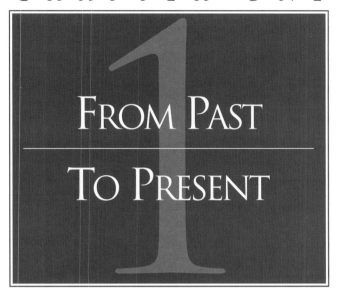

FROM PAST
TO PRESENT

A PLACE WITH PROMISE

◆

"Tallahassee continues to struggle to maintain its beauty, small-town feel, and friendly character as it grows into a larger city that faces twenty-first century problems."

–Penny Shaw Herman,
Mayor of Tallahassee

◆

Today's new Tallahasseeans come in search of something more—a place with promise—someplace they can embrace and call home. Photo by Robert M. Overton.

A reverence for history and a hope for the future; a contrast between the "old" and "new" Florida; a push for progress in territories paved by the past. Perched atop one of Tallahassee's highest hills, the close proximity of the Old and the New Capitol is one of the best examples of how the past and the present can complement each other. Photo by Robert M. Overton.

Sitting in our comfortable, air-conditioned homes, it's hard to imagine what possessed a small party of seven ever to brave the raw frontier of 1824 and set up camp in Tallahassee. Back then, the underbrush was probably inter-woven as tight as wool threads in a winter throw, mosquitos most likely grew to the size of clenched fists, and the heat and humidity so intense they grabbed your breath and kept it for days. Ralph Waldo Emerson disliked his 1827 visit so much that he described Tallahassee as "a grotesque place . . . rapidly settled by public officers, land speculators, and desperadoes."

Yet the wild and spirited character of early Tallahassee con-tinued to attract settlers. A few were drawn to opportunities in the newly created capital city, but most simply came in search of something more. A place with promise. Someplace better

Tallahassee's magnetic attraction is expected to grow with the recent addition of the nation's top center for research in magnet-related technologies, the National High Magnetic Field Laboratory. Photo by Robert M. Overton.

than where they came from. Someplace they could embrace and call home.

Like their counterparts of 170 years ago, today's new Tallahasseeans are drawn by the same reasons. They want relief from the squeeze of big city life. They want room to breathe and uncrowded space to discover and explore. They want to be recognized as a single voice, not just part of a background chorus.

Oh, there are still a few public officers, land speculators, and desperadoes hanging around, but for the most part, Tallahasseeans constantly strive to make this a better place than it already is, to work together for a community that reflects the spirit and determination of our forefathers. Our history has made us what we are in the present, a vibrant community with the resilience to recover from misfortunes and cope with constant changes. There is an appreciation for the past, but even more, there is cognizance of a shared future.

Glimpses of our growing city can be found in almost every sector. Government jobs continue to be an economic mainstay, comprising 40 percent of Tallahassee's workforce, yet small business owners are finding that Tallahassee is the ideal incubator for a new business.

Advanced technology is now commonplace in the community, and with the addition of the National High Magnetic Field Laboratory, other high-tech industries are giving Tallahassee a second glance.

As always, the stimulating and dynamic atmospheres of two distinguished universities, Florida State University and Florida Agricultural and Mechanical University, keep a spotlight directed toward our city. Tallahassee Community College, created in 1966, is also coming into its own.

Revitalization of the downtown area, architecturally as well as economically, has rejuvenated the tired, dated side of our city. In the outskirts, growth continues commercially and residentially.

It's hard to imagine what possessed a small party of seven ever to brave the raw frontier and set up camp in Tallahassee. Yet the wild and spirited character of early Tallahassee continued to attract settlers. Photo by Robert M. Overton.

The stimulating atmospheres of two distinguished universities keep a spotlight directed toward our city. Being part of a major educational mecca also means major opportunities. Photo by Robert M. Overton.

And to balance this growth and provide a haven for both business and the natural environment, city planners have implemented plans to protect the beauty we've been blessed with. As William Warren Rogers, FSU history professor, said, "We'd better protect what we have because we're light years ahead of those places that start with nothing."

Our city is undergoing a metamorphosis. Changes in outlook, technology, and direction have blended to create a Tallahassee that makes the most of a rich past while looking forward to an even brighter future. There is a fusion of old Southern charm with New South progressiveness.

Now, closer in time to the twenty-first century than to that wild and untamed period of 1824, our growing city stands in sharp contrast to the days of its infancy. Regardless, the ideals and dreams that brought people to Tallahassee in the past will undoubtedly continue to bring them here in the future. ◆

—Heidi Tyline King

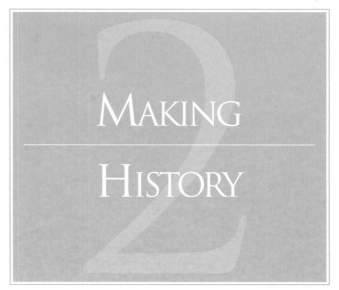

MAKING

HISTORY

OLD SOUTHERN CHARM, NEW SOUTH PROGRESSIVENESS

◆

"We should aim to maintain everything that's good about the past but be revitalized by the present."

–William Warren Rogers,
Professor of History,
Florida State University

◆

Before its existence as a state capital, Tallahassee was a principal village for Indians who hunted the land, fished the waters, and eventually became farmers. Photo by Robert M. Overton.

Artifacts found at de Soto's winter camp suggest the area probably was the site of the main Apalachee town where the explorer and his followers settled in October 1539. Presently, the site is the only confirmed de Soto camp in North America, and ironically it is located less than a mile from the Capitol. Photo by Robert M. Overton.

Tallahassee's history is no more than a jigsaw puzzle of places, events, and people. Separately, each piece represents merely a fragment of what came before—de Soto, the Civil War, the Apalachee Trail. Yet when interlocked, the pieces combine to create a colorful mosaic of the present, a complete picture of the Tallahassee we know today.

Geologically speaking, Tallahassee's red hills originally came from Georgia and the Appalachian foothills. The Big Bend area, like the rest of Florida, spent most of its early days under water. Over time, layers of sand and other sediments carried by northern streams collected on the limestone foundation of the ocean floor, and when the seas subsided, the red clay hills of Tallahassee and the flat, sandy plains of the coastal lowlands slowly emerged.

Much later, nomadic Indian tribes from the north and the west migrated to Florida, subsisting temporarily in one location, then moving to another when the area's food supply was depleted. Their descendants, the Apalachees, also hunted and fished, but they eventually became farmers, planting and harvesting domesticated crops such as corn, beans, and squash. Farming supplemented their diet, yet more importantly, it was instrumental in the Apalachees' transition from a nomadic to a more sedentary lifestyle.

Prosperous years followed and the Apalachees evolved into a highly advanced civilization, with trade routes stretching the entire continent. Goods were traded with tribes as far north as Minnesota and as far south, as some archaeologists believe, as South America. Consequently, Tallahassee quickly became a regional center for the area's commerce, and social, political, and economic systems grew increasingly complex.

Early explorers visited Apalachee territory as early as 1528, but it wasn't until 1539 that Hernando de Soto led 600 men to the area in search of purported riches. De Soto's winter camp has long been thought to be the site of the first Christmas Mass in North America, a theory supported by the 1987 discovery of brass chainmail, coins, pig bones, and pottery shards dating the present-day site to that particular time period.

Sometime before 1656, two Franciscan missions were established in Tallahassee by missionaries from the Spanish settlement at Saint Augustine. At times, relations between the two groups were strained, but the missions continued to grow, and the population of both Spaniards and Christianized Indians had steadily increased by the end of the seventeenth century.

In the 1700s, France and England began claiming large sections of land in and around Florida, joining Spain in the quest for administrative control of the territory. Rivalries soon turned into a series of wars, and Florida flip-flopped between Spanish and English rule throughout much of the century.

The most devastating blow for the Apalachees came in 1704, when Governor James Moore of South Carolina led an

English military expedition against the mission settlements. Moore's troops destroyed the missions, and those Indians who weren't murdered were captured, sold into slavery in the Carolinas, or relocated on the Oconee River in Georgia. The entire Apalachee population was virtually wiped out.

It was over a hundred years later before Florida became a territory of the newly formed United States. In 1821 President James Monroe appointed Andrew Jackson the provisional or military governor, a position he held for 80 days before resigning and returning to his Tennessee home. William Pope DuVal became the first territorial governor in 1822.

The cities of Saint Augustine and Pensacola were flourishing, but the distance between the two made it increasingly difficult for the legislative council to meet. As a compromise, Governor DuVal appointed Dr. William H. Simmons of Saint Augustine and John Lee Williams of Pensacola to explore the area between the Ochlocknee and Suwannee Rivers to find a suitable place for a permanent capital. Williams finally persuaded Simmons to agree upon the site of an old Indian village, Tallahassee, meaning "old town" or "old fields."

Just as the Indians who came centuries before, settlers from across the Southeast soon arrived, attracted by Tallahassee's rich, fertile soils and abundant wildlife and vegetation. The population grew from the first party of seven that arrived in 1824 to the state's most populous county with more than 11,500 occupants by 1845, when Florida became a state and Tallahassee the official state capital.

Ironically, Tallahassee is one of the few cities in the United States specifically created to serve as a state capital. On the eve of the Civil War, Tallahassee had been transformed from a sleepy, backwoods town into a bustling society, due in part to wealthy planters from the North who had brought their sophisticated lifestyles with them.

Nevertheless, secession was at hand, and in January 1861, Tallahassee hosted the secession convention where Florida became the third state to secede from the Union. With the outbreak of the

Civil War, almost 1,500 of Leon County's men enlisted in Confederate forces. About 15,000 Floridians fought for the Confederate States, most participating in war efforts much farther north. Florida also had approximately 1,200 white soldiers fight for the Union and almost as many blacks.

As the state capital, Tallahassee was the base for all of Florida's war activity, and the state as a whole provided vital support to the Confederate cause. Even so, Florida was not considered a major threat in the war, and the closest combat to Tallahassee was the Battle of Natural Bridge near Saint Marks. Florida's secessionist efforts ended May 20, 1865, with the defeat of the Confederate army, and the state was put under military control. Tallahassee was the only state capital east of the Mississippi that did not fall to the Union during the Civil War.

The Reconstruction Period following the war was a time of readjustment for the state and its capital city. Political parties clashed as tax structures were revamped, public schools were created, and blacks were given the right to vote. For awhile,

GROUP C. O. AND STAFF

Dale Mabry Field was selected as a subbase of McDill Field at Tampa by the Army Air Corps in 1940, serving as an aviation training facility for combat fighter pilots. Photo courtesy of the Florida State Archives.

agriculture remained the basis of the local economy, but diversified to crops other than cotton.

In the 1880s the extensive plantation system spreading across Leon County and into south Georgia was revived—not by Southerners—but by Northerners who turned the land into prime hunting ground for quail. These winter "hunting lodges" or "shooting plantations" virtually ended Leon County's reign as Florida's top agricultural county, and native farmers began moving out of the country and into Tallahassee.

Despite its population of less than 20,000 people at the turn of the century, Leon County weathered various economic and political shifts and capitalized upon its position as state capital and the home of two higher institutions of education. The city also managed to counter talk of moving the capital from Tallahassee. The first attempt was actually made before the

Civil War, but Tallahasseeans won the vote in a statewide referendum. Later, in 1900, a statewide vote kept the capital in Tallahassee.

During this time, modern conveniences such as electricity, city sewage, telephones, and automobiles made their way to the city, and cultural activities thrived, including those related to local colleges.

Although Tallahassee and Leon County felt the crunch of the Great Depression, the slow, steady growth of the 1920s prevented them from facing total devastation. Unlike the rest of Florida, they did not experience the boom of the '20s, and they did not suffer as much during the financial crisis.

Not quite a hundred years after the Civil War, Tallahassee once more came to the aid of her country, this time the United States. A steady stream of men answered the call to service, Dale Mabry Field became an aviation training facility for combat fighter pilots, and students from Florida State College for Women and Florida Agricultural and Mechanical College volunteered for the cause.

The postwar era saw a boom in population, and by 1960 Tallahassee had over 48,000 occupants. Both colleges grew into universities, Tallahassee Community College was created, and businesses prospered.

The '50s and '60s also heralded the Civil Rights Movement as blacks struggled for equal rights. Sit-ins by FAMU students were staged and bus boycotts were instituted. Although racial relations were lacking, there was no massive resistance to black demands, and Tallahassee somehow managed to survive the era with little violence.

Today, Tallahassee's economy no longer depends on agriculture, but continues to rely upon the governmental and educational centers as major sources of employment and income. Population growth has steadily increased, as well as private businesses and nonprofit associations. As the twenty-first century nears, the city is preparing itself for the future, a future that will certainly face the problems that come with urbanization, but one that will be rooted deep in the accomplishments and pride of the past. ◆

—Heidi Tyline King

Although racial relations were lacking, there was no massive resistance to the black demands, and Tallahassee somehow managed to survive the Civil Rights Movement of the '50s and '60s with little violence. Photo courtesy of the Florida State Archives.

CHAPTER THREE

BUSINESS
CLIMATE

TRADITIONAL PAST, HIGH-TECH FUTURE

◆

"Tallahassee is a 'capital city' in many ways, epitomizing the dynamic quality of the State of Florida in its evolution from a small settlement to a thriving agricultural town to a present-day metropolis."

–Excerpt from
Tallahassee, Favored Land

◆

Tallahassee is the capital city of one of the fastest growing states in the nation. Employment is dominated by government with over 40 percent of the workforce employed in municipal, state, and federal jobs. Photo by Robert M. Overton.

An artist drawing the skyline of Tallahassee might depict bushy, moss-draped oak trees cozying up to stately looking brick structures, interspersed with historic homes-turned-professional-offices. Somewhere in its landscape would be the domed Capitol building and a cluster of state office buildings in the surrounding complex.

This is what surprises visitors most when they come to Tallahassee. They don't see towering buildings standing shoulder-to-shoulder. There are no skyscrapers or smokestacks. Instead, in this attractive north Florida location they discover businesses in harmony with canopied roads and other Old South features.

The picture Tallahassee paints for itself seems somehow to hide the business talent located in this resource-rich community. That's not to say it's not here. After all, Tallahassee is the capital city of one of the fastest growing states in the nation. Florida has been a national pacesetter in new business incorporations, leading the nation six out of the last seven years in total numbers.

PROFILE OF A CITY

With a base population of 245,000, according to the 1992 census figures, the metropolitan area continues to grow with more than 3,000 people migrating to Leon County each year. The majority of newcomers are relatively young, affluent, well-educated, and skilled. Over 40 percent of Leon County's residents are between the ages of 25 and 49, and the median age is 29.

Tallahassee has historically enjoyed a stable, but growing, economy. Employment is dominated by government with over 40 percent of the workforce employed in municipal, state, and federal jobs. A large percentage of the remaining employed owe their livelihood to small business. State and national associations, light manufacturing operations, and regional distribution centers have also found Tallahassee a superior location and represent a growing employment sector.

But larger employers in the health care services field and an increased concentration of research facilities are combining to create spinoffs of both industry and opportunity.

Tallahassee Memorial Regional Medical Center is the area's largest nongovernmental employer (it's actually a private/public partnership). Publix supermarkets is the next highest. Other large private employers following in suit are Sprint/Centel-Florida, Wal-Mart, and the Tallahassee Community Hospital.

FAST-GROWING SMALL BUSINESS SECTOR

In an independent survey released in 1993, Tallahassee was judged "an entrepreneurial hot spot," one of the best places in America to start a company. And for good reason.

There are stories of small businesses making their mark in Tallahassee. Take International Research Bureau (IRB), for

The attractiveness of GTO as a citizen of Tallahassee is how clean the manufacturing process is and how committed the company is to the city. Zinc, steel, and plastic remnants are recycled to become raw materials. Virtually all of each operator's parts are manufactured at GTO's facility. Photo by Robert M. Overton.

instance. The locally owned and operated private investigation agency took their 2-employee operation from a family garage to a 25-employee firm occupying a two-story office building in a little over five years.

Specializing in locating missing people, conducting preemployment background checks, and finding assets, the company was honored with the Tallahassee Area Chamber of Commerce's 1992 Export Business of the Year award.

Like IRB, smaller and middle-sized firms producing the most growth and innovation prefer to start companies in communities with universities, interstate highways, airports, advanced telecommunications, and a positive entrepreneurial culture—that's Tallahassee.

Another company capitalizing on the area's resources is GTO, Inc., which began the production and sales of the first do-it-yourself automatic gate openers in 1987. The company is now the largest manufacturer of do-it-yourself solar-powered gate operators in the world, and its "Mighty Mule" brand is the only one sold through the retail market.

GTO was also recognized for its achievement. It received the State of Florida's Governor's New Product Award in 1993 and ranked 167 on *Inc.* magazine's list of "500 Fastest Growing Private Companies in the United States."

It recently expanded facilities in Commonwealth Centre, an office, industrial, and corporate research park and is projecting sales of $12.1 million in 1995.

FOUNDATIONS TO BUILD ON

General Dynamics Land Systems Division, which manufactures single-channel ground and airborne radios (SINCGARS) and light electronics, mostly for the defense industry, is one of Tallahassee's earlier economic development success stories. The company was enticed to the area in 1987 by an existing building and a favorable environment for establishing operations in Commonwealth Centre. Area business and political leaders formed a partnership to create optimal conditions for negotiations. General Dynamics has continued to deliver on its promise to bring jobs to Tallahassee, and has since gained varying contracts to keep the manufacturing operation at capacity.

Discreetly tucked away in a 96,000-square-foot facility, with its sister operation, Talla-Com, located in nearby Innovation Park, General Dynamics is responsible for over 500 jobs. At full operational level, it expects to have a total of 700. Combined, the operations had a payroll of $12.2 million in 1993, and projected payrolls of $15.9 million in 1994, and $16.6 million in 1995.

In order to keep business and government agencies on the cutting edge of information processing, Sprint/Centel established an ultra-sophisticated fiber-optic highway, called a "Metropolitan Area Network." State agencies can now pass volumes of data back and forth in seconds. Photo by Robert M. Overton.

In addition to light manufacturing, service industries are an important employer in the Tallahassee area. Tallahassee is home to a myriad of membership organizations, legal and business services firms.

The Florida Chamber of Commerce, the largest state chamber of commerce in the country and Florida's largest broad-based business organization, is located in downtown Tallahassee. Like other membership-based associations, the Chamber finds special benefits to doing business from an area that's a political anchor for the state, including legislative integration with other association functions, networking with legislative and regulatory staff, and an optimal environment for communications.

Companies searching for viable distribution locations have found attractive features in Tallahassee and Leon County as well. Coca-Cola recently expanded to a new 17,000-square-foot regional distribution center in Commonwealth. Company officials cited the park's location advantage, next to Interstate 10, as making it easier to get in, out, and around Tallahassee.

Other companies with regional distribution centers operating out of Commonwealth include Domino's Pizza, Dyke Industries, and Stanadyne Automotive.

HIGH-TECH ASSETS

Because it's the seat of state government, Tallahassee is also the computer capital of Florida. In fact, more than half of Florida's computer power is situated in Tallahassee.

In order to keep these networks connected and keep business and government agencies on the cutting edge of information processing, the local telephone company, Sprint/Centel, established an ultra-sophisticated fiber-optic highway, called

For its size, Tallahassee has a larger than average concentration of health care facilities, serving residents of north Florida and south Georgia as both a regional medical center and health care training source. Photo by Ray Stanyard.

a "Metropolitan Area Network" or MAN, which encircles the downtown area.

Tallahassee now leads the way in state-of-the-art telecommunications with its fiber-optic networks which accommodate high speed voice, data, and image transmission and teleconferencing.

State agencies use the MAN mostly to send volumes of data back and forth to each other. They can do things in hours that it used to take days to do. In the past, they had to copy information onto a tape or disk and overnight it or run it by carriers. Now, through fiber optics, they can transmit data in seconds 24 hours a day.

Fiber optics help power the growth of companies like Fringe Benefits Management Company which serves a national customer base from this central north Florida location.

Fringe Benefits, which sells and services fringe benefits management systems to public employers, is one of Tallahassee's many business success stories. The company has 178,000 customers (as of July 1994) scattered across the United States with nearly 240 employees. Their revenues have tripled from under 3 million per annum to over 12 million and are projected to triple again by 1997.

The company was selected as a regional first place recipient of the Governor's Annual Business Leadership Award in 1993. They were nominated based on the company's progressive management style and its implementation of innovative

programs such as quality assurance, recycling, and drug-free workplace initiatives.

ANSWERING THE CONSUMER DEMAND

Tallahassee has gained a growing reputation for its vast consumer market. Big chain stores are clamoring to serve the population with a healthy median household effective buying income of over $28,900.

The northeast part of town, where much of the residential growth has occurred in the past 10 years, gained a burst of retail centers in 1994. Lowe's moved into a new and expanded location within months of Home Depot's opening and is located less than a mile away from the competitor. Tallahassee's northwest quadrant has also scored high in retail stores with a growing number of strip shopping centers anchored by major grocery tenants. The southside is gearing up for redevelopment as well, and it appears that businesses desiring closer proximity to downtown will find it inviting.

POSITIONED FOR EVEN STRONGER GROWTH

In four of the past six years, the state of Florida has ranked number one in new plants and expansions, and Tallahassee is positioning itself to get a larger share of that economic development pie.

Tallahassee ranks strong in areas at the top of virtually every site-selector's check off list for relocating or expanding business. Features most appealing include the following: a network of health care providers; a highly skilled, underemployed workforce; enormous educational opportunities (Tallahassee has two state universities, a community college, and a vocational school); a world renowned location for research with the National High Magnetic Field Laboratory; a city-owned multiuse business park and state-owned research park; and a recently expanded $32-million regional airport with room to accommodate growth.

HEALTH CARE PROVIDERS

For its size, Tallahassee has a larger than average concentration of health care facilities, and industry predictors say this fact positions the city for increasing opportunities in the future.

Tallahassee serves residents of north Florida and south Georgia as both a regional medical center and health care training source.

There are currently two full-service acute-care facilities: Tallahassee Memorial Regional Medical Center, a 771-bed hospital, and Tallahassee Community Hospital, a 180-bed hospital. HEALTHSOUTH Rehabilitation Hospital of Tallahassee provides comprehensive inpatient and outpatient programs in the areas of brain injury, spinal cord injury, stroke, orthopedics, amputations, arthritis, and pain management. The Arbors at

Tallahassee is a rehabilitation and subacute center offering a full range of rehab services for patients discharged from a hospital but unable to return to their homes immediately.

In addition, Tallahassee offers a full range of outpatient surgical centers, including Tallahassee Single Day Surgery. Other facilities in the community provide diagnostic imaging, including X-ray, ultrasound, mammography, computed tomography (CAT scans), and magnetic resonance imaging (MRIs), and complete laboratory services on an inpatient/outpatient basis.

There are two comprehensive mental health centers—the Apalachee Center for Human Services and the Psychiatric Center at Tallahassee Memorial—in addition to the many psychiatrists, psychologists, counselors, and mental health professionals.

Physical therapy is well represented with 18 clinics currently serving patients. Chiropractic services are also widely accessible. There are a growing number of home health care companies serving patients in the area.

A strong managed care presence in Tallahassee has helped keep the cost of health care benefits down for employers. In addition to the availability of traditional preferred provider organizations (PPOs), health maintenance organizations (HMOs) are a popular choice. Hundreds of area physicians, hospitals, and numerous allied health professionals participate in the area's managed care networks.

AVAILABILITY OF QUALIFIED LABOR

Tallahassee has a well-educated population which provides an exceptionally skilled workforce for local employers. The 1990 census reported the percentage of the population with at least four years of college increased to 41 percent from 1980 to 1990—a 9 percent jump—which is well above the state average of 18 percent.

Career advancement and professional development opportunities are endless with Florida State University (FSU), Florida Agricultural and Mechanical University (FAMU), Tallahassee Community College (TCC), and Lively Technical Center, all based in Tallahassee. The combined enrollment of the four schools is over 59,000 students.

Historically, Tallahassee has enjoyed a comparably low unemployment rate of around three percent. The low unemployment rate has led some companies with their eyes on Tallahassee mistakenly to believe that the area offered a limited labor pool from which to draw. But a recent survey of graduates showed that universities are manufacturing a high quality labor force that is not tapped to its fullest potential.

In the study, more than two-thirds of graduates from FSU said they would remain in Tallahassee if offered employment in their fields. Sixty-three percent of respondents from FAMU indicated they would stay in the area if offered jobs in their career fields,

also. And a phenomenal 39 percent of FSU graduates and 21 percent of FAMU graduates said they would like to remain in Tallahassee based on quality of life, alone.

The study gave evidence to a common theory among economic development professionals: graduates often accept jobs that are less than their degrees qualify them for, to take advantage of the quality of life Tallahassee offers.

The bottom line is that people love Tallahassee and want to stay, even if it means lowering their career expectations. Although this may not sound like good news to most people, it's dynamic news for potential employers, as they're assured of finding both an eager and qualified workforce.

RICH IN RESOURCES

With the light now shining on Tallahassee's unique predicament, political, business, and community leaders are committing themselves to create not just jobs, but better paying jobs for citizens in the future.

One of the assets predicted to spur that growth is Tallahassee's abundant resources for research and high technology. More companies are discovering the benefits of a world-renowned location rich in resources for research, two state universities, numerous regional health care facilities, a highly skilled, underemployed workforce, and two publicly-owned office, industrial, and corporate research parks.

The magnetic attraction is expected to grow with the recent addition of the nation's top center for research in magnet-related

Home to two major universities and a thriving community college, potential employers are assured to find both an eager and qualified workforce in Tallahassee. Photo courtesy of Florida A&M University. Photo by Keith Pope.

technologies, the National High Magnetic Field Laboratory. Because the prestigious Mag Lab is expected to be fully operational by 1995, the area is predicted to be an origin for many of the next century's scientific discoveries and emerging technologies. That spells good news for industry. Tallahassee will

Commonwealth Centre comprises 440 total acres of construction-ready lots. Seaboard Coast Line Railroad forms the eastern boundary, providing rail access, and the Tallahassee/Leon County Regional Airport is just five miles away. Photo by Robert M. Overton.

be in a unique position to benefit from the work of Nobel Prize-winning scientists.

Operated by a consortium composed of Florida State University, the University of Florida, and the Los Alamos National Laboratory, this national user facility is open to qualified scientists from government, academia, and industry. Over 400 teams of national and international scientists are expected to conduct publishable research each year, which will expand the scientific base in Tallahassee and encourage high technology companies to establish operations here.

Tallahassee already is receiving enormous national attention from high-tech corporations interested in establishing offices near the facility, which is located in Innovation Park.

One of the key components of locating the lab in Tallahassee was the fact that Tallahassee and the state of Florida have the resources readily available for high-tech industries. Those resources include people with the knowledge and capabilities to handle advanced equipment and research.

With the increasing interest nationwide for technology transfer programs and university/private-sector partnerships, Tallahassee is positioned to be at the forefront for identifying and commercially developing new technologies. Fields with promising opportunities include high field magnetics, medical and biomedical technology, advanced materials research, software technology, transportation systems, aerospace technologies, advanced communications, and educational materials/technology.

Research facilities in Tallahassee which are expected to play a role in the commercialization of products, processes, and ideas include Supercomputer Computations Research Institute at Florida State University. Recognized internationally for its research accomplishments in physics, chemistry, materials science, biological science, and the geosciences, the Supercomputer Computations Research Institute (SCRI) has attracted an international group of 40 scientists in a variety of disciplines that use higher-performance computers, creating a unique interdisciplinary research institute.

SCRI maintains two of the world's fastest and most powerful supercomputers. It ranks among the world's leaders in using today's super-powerful, super-fast computers to push the limits of science and technology. The institute comprises more than four dozen researchers who combine talents to study enormously complex problems in a score of scientific fields. Industrial collaborators find SCRI to be an excellent extension of their home facilities with its office space, computers, world-wide network connections, and consultants with a large range of scientific and computational expertise.

New technologies emerging in fields such as medicine, computing, aerospace engineering, transportation, textile manufacturing, communication, and bioengineering are being made possible by rapid advancement in a single area of basic research: materials science.

One of the nation's fastest-growing centers for material research, the Center for Materials Research and Technology (MARTECH), was established by the Florida legislature in 1985. It has emerged as the Southeast's premier facility for advanced research in several materials science fields.

Faculty of the FAMU/FSU College of Engineering are actively engaged in research in such diverse areas as structural analysis of bridges and highways, tides in coastal rivers, heat exchanges, robotics, superconductors, laser beam propagation through water, aerodynamics, high temperature superconducting materials, controls, aeroacoustics, intelligent manufacturing processes, molecular engineering, chemical and biochemical processes, digital signal processes, and computer integrated manufacturing.

By collaborating with industry on research, product development, and professional service, the FAMU/FSU College of Engineering hopes to have a positive impact on the state and national economy.

LOCATIONAL ASSETS

Communities competing for economic development would consider the availability of an industrial park a popular feature on their list of assets. A municipally-owned park would be even better. The fact that Tallahassee has not one—but two—gives

Tallahassee's new $32-million regional airport offers numerous daily flights on jet carriers plus commuter lines. Photo by Robert M. Overton.

this area a strong advantage for business expansion opportunities.

Commonwealth Centre, located adjacent to Interstate 10 and Capital Circle Northwest—Tallahassee's major truck route—comprises 440 total acres with city-owned lots which are construction-ready. Seaboard Coast Line Railroad forms the eastern boundary, providing rail access, and the Tallahassee/ Leon County Regional Airport is just five miles away.

Although many parks are located on the outskirts of town, Commonwealth Centre is minutes away from a major shopping district. The FAMU/FSU College of Engineering, both university campuses, the community college, and the vocational-technical school are also in close proximity, making labor and training more accessible.

Innovation Park/Tallahassee is a research and development center that was created by state legislation to encourage the collaboration and transfer of technology between the two affiliated universities—Florida State University and Florida A&M University—government laboratories, and private industry.

Encompassing 208 acres, the activities concentrated there are research, product development, testing, education, and scientifically-oriented production or product assembly.

The park is governed by the Leon County Research & Development Authority and offers build-to-suit facilities for organizations with competitive rates utilizing tax-exempt funding and scientific activity ad valorem tax exemptions. The park also offers unique financial incentives for qualified tenants.

TRANSPORTATION A PLUS

Tallahassee counts among its many business-friendly features the ready accessibility by air and multiple highway routes.

The city is bisected by four major federal highways—U.S. 90, U.S. 27, U.S. 319, and Interstate 10. The center of the city is located only 90 minutes from Interstate 75, the corridor linking northern states to Florida.

And Tallahassee's new $32-million regional airport offers numerous daily flights on jet carriers plus commuter lines. Charter, private, and air cargo services are also available.

Amtrak's Sunset Limited, a transcontinental route from Los Angeles to Miami, includes a stop in Tallahassee. Rail freight is available through CSX, and 11 motor freight carriers with local terminal facilities make shipping easier for business.

A CLIMATE THAT MEANS BUSINESS

Important to any company is the availability of a support system through economic development and business groups. Tallahassee has a strong Chamber of Commerce and Economic Development Council. The Chamber's concerted effort has helped cultivate a very supportive and progressive leadership within the city and county political structures.

Concentrating efforts on servicing the existing business base and marketing the area's business climate for expanding industries, the Tallahassee Chamber and its members are helping to preserve Tallahassee and Leon County's economic vitality while assuring an unparalleled quality of life for its citizens. ◆

—Julie S. Bettinger

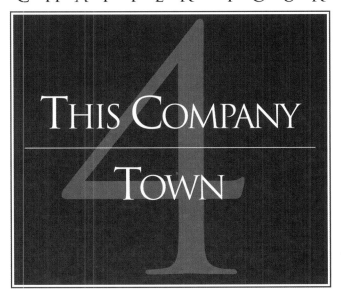

THIS COMPANY TOWN

4

OF SENATORS AND STATE WORKERS

◆

*"Old capitol, old dowager hinting
of her former years; awnings
lipstick red, cosmetic ornament
adorning raw ambition...
Old capitol, blushing courtesan
now granted restoration stands
in her mortar shawl of gray
beneath the shadow of her
towering progeny and in the
ancient shades displays the
splendid dowry of her lusty,
homespun past."*

–From *Meridian Markers*
by Barbara Gene Fisher

◆

*Candy stripe awnings adorn the Old Capitol, which is now a part of the
Museum of Florida History, and offers exhibits on the state's political
and social development. Photo by Robert M. Overton.*

Lawmaking and comradeship proliferated in the halls of The Floridan Hotel when the legislature was in session. Demolished in 1985, the hotel played hostess to many grand affairs and political powwows during its heyday. Photo courtesy of the Florida State Archives.

"There's more offered here than just the three-percent raise I get," Adams says. The benefits are good and opportunities are bountiful, "if you seize them," he clarifies.

Among them, he says, are health, life, and dental insurance; deferred compensation; and educational opportunities. Adams says he's asked himself the question before: "If I give this up to go to the private sector—how much do I have to make to replace it?"

He recently decided to take better advantage of the state perks and is now seeking a master's in public health on the state's prepaid tuition program.

Adams gets a lot of personal satisfaction from his job, too. Comparing what he does for the state and what he might be doing for a corporation, he says, "It's a difference of asking yourself, 'What did I accomplish today?' and you answer either 'Today I made stockholders money,' or 'Today I might have saved a child's life.'"

Another perk is the ability to move up or out—to another agency. Once you're in the system, it's easier to move around, Adams says. State workers have a clear advantage for attaining other state jobs because job announcements are circulated among staff. And most insiders know how to assure they're given strong consideration for the job.

To get a foot in the door, a lot of people are willing to accept temporary positions with no benefits, called "OPS"—an acronym which stands for "Other Personal Services." OPS is a way to get noticed so that when a permanent job opens up, the employee has an established history, by state standards.

KNOWING THE LINGO

A knowledge of the inner workings of state government is a plus in this town, even if you're an outsider it seems. And knowledge gained on the inside can give you an edge.

Claude Pichard has worked for the Florida Department of Law Enforcement (FDLE) for five years, and he admits it took him a while to catch on. "It took me probably two to two and a half years from the time I came here to really understand how state government works—because it's a completely different animal from private industry. You really have to think of things in a different manner and change the way you do a lot of things. There's a learning curve to it; it takes you a while to figure out how the system works. It's a good system for the most part, but it's different."

And if you don't have the advantage of knowing the system, he says, it's wise to surround yourself with people who have a history with the state and know the procedures.

Hired as a producer/director for the video section of FDLE, Pichard is now a research and training specialist. He coordinates media relations classes for the department, traveling the state to instruct sheriffs' deputies, chiefs of police, and law enforcement public information officers on how to deal with the media. He says the knowledge he's gained working in the state system will serve him for a lifetime.

When he was working with the private sector prior to his state job, Pichard says, "The few times I would have to call the state I would be completely lost—I would have no idea who to call and what to ask for. It was this huge bureaucracy, and I had no idea where to start—but now I do. A lot of the state agencies' structures are similar, and I know who should take care of this thing or that."

"I call it the back channels," agrees David Adams. "Normally you would write a memo, give out nine copies—in triplicate. But if you know the system, you can make a phone call first and say, 'This is the idea we've got,' get a yes or no, and it saves you a lot of time."

THE LEGISLATURE IS "IN"

"Once [and not too many years ago] it came with the force of a huge wave, engulfed the community, and swept aside other interests . . . . The town filled up and overflowed with legislators, lobbyists, attachés, and even a flurry of ordinary spectators . . . . It was Tallahassee's 'season,' almost as much as the tourist season that sustained the economy of south Florida cities."

This description, excerpted from the late Malcolm B. Johnson's book *I Declare!,* tells a tale of the old days of Florida's legislature. This particular column, "Town Absorbs the Legislature," was published April 2, 1974.

Johnson, a former newspaper columnist with the *Tallahassee Democrat,* continues: "All eyes in Tallahassee stayed on the Legislature while it was in session, and every morning brought a new run of gossip about what had gone on the night before at the few steak houses [jukes] and road houses where politicians gathered and relaxed. Downtown was still downtown, and most of us couldn't stay away from it for fear of missing something . . . ."

"We hardly notice the Legislature, in regular session, nowadays. It comes and goes annually instead of biennially, and its members come once a month most of the year for several days of committee hearings."

"In the Capitol, the legislators go about their business almost overlooked by the residents of Tallahassee. 'The session' is no less bread and butter to this state-owned city than it ever was, but it flows and ebbs with more urbanity in a more urbane setting than it did even 20 years ago."

It's true. Politics has helped shape Tallahassee since the city was chosen as the territorial capital in 1823. In the fall of 1824, the legislative council, which had been meeting alternately in Pensacola and Saint Augustine, first met in a pine log cabin located on the southeast part of the Capitol Square, according to historical accounts.

"Official state business" conducted today is a stark contrast to earlier accounts, though. Legislators and their influencers meet in the much more polished halls of the bustling Capitol building—a 22-story tower, flanked by domes. Policy makers officially convene once or more a year, to enact laws and adopt a state budget during legislative and special sessions.

Today's legislature is vastly different from its predecessor. A new breed of lobbyists—who battle it out on behalf of clients—is armed with information and knowledge of the process. Photo by Robert M. Overton.

Earlier accounts of lawmaking—often called "the good old days"—still surface on occasion. It was a time when taking care of business meant using a smaller, less complicated structure (though many question its fairness by today's standards).

HE KNOWS OF THOSE DAYS

Mallory Horne, now chairman of the Public Employees Relation Commission, was an up-and-coming legislator in the early 1960s. As he tells it, the city of Tallahassee offered few places for meeting and entertaining between lobbyists and legislators other than The Floridan Hotel. "If you went anywhere in Tallahassee—it was The Floridan," Horne says.

Demolished in 1985, The Floridan played hostess to grand affairs and political powwows when there was little else for senators and representatives in this company town.

Lawmaking and comradeship proliferated in the halls of the hotel when the legislature was in session. "If you wanted anything done, it was done at The Floridan for the most part," says Horne. "It became, during those three months, 'the other capitol.'" They only passed laws officially at the Capitol building.

Government in the Sunshine had not taken effect, and Horne says lobbyists gathered at The Floridan and agreed to pass a bill; appropriations and conference committees would meet—"Then they'd close up the room and just do it," he says.

One of the few people who held positions as both the Speaker of the House and President of the Senate during his political career, Horne recalls elegant dining and a lot of fancy private parties in the old hotel.

The cabinet entertained there, as did the governors. It was "the" place for inaugural parties. Lobbyists paid for elaborate food, and it was "a center for the sublime to the ridiculous, because there really wasn't anything else in Tallahassee," Horne says.

Being a one-hotel town contributed to the argument to relocate the capital to Orlando which erupted in the late 1950s. The fact that the city was dry was another contention. Leon County didn't allow legal sales of liquor by package until 1960 and by the drink until 1967. For politicians coming from more cosmopolitan parts, that was an inconvenience. (Even though there was an unspoken agreement among law enforcers in Tallahassee's earlier days to look the other way when bootlegged liquor arrived in quantities at The Floridan.)

A town of less than 40,000 people in the post World War II days, Tallahassee was still rather laid back, and legislators contended there was little to do, no places to stay, and definitely nothing here to keep their families entertained during the long weeks of the session.

By 1966, when the fight had come to a head, nearly 60 percent of the voting power was from central Florida, south. Things didn't look good. But Tallahassee area business leaders committed to work together to create the type of climate legislators were look-ing for: places that accommodated families, restaurants to gather in, and an expanded Capitol facility.

Still, everything was pretty shaky until around 1968, when legislators agreed to stick with the capital's original home. "Following that, Tallahassee began to be what it is now, with real alternatives for family," Horne says.

A DIFFERENT WORLD TODAY

Often fodder for newspaper editorials, the relationship of lobbyists and legislators is frequently and cynically questioned by the public. In earlier days, maybe, but the 1990s legislature is vastly different from its predecessor.

Art Collins, a 34-year-old lobbyist and president of Public Private Partnership, represents the new breed of lobbyists—battling it out on behalf of his clients armed with information, rather than expensive bottles of wine or hefty expense accounts.

New reforms are in place to keep legislative practices aboveboard. Still, Collins says, "It's very easy to be cynical on the outside."

The public usually hears about the scandals, and a lot of times they think that's the essence—"shaking hands and making deals"—but he says nothing could be further from the truth. "It's a serious, tough business, and there are a lot of good, sincere people here trying to do the right thing."

In addition to curbs on lobbyist-legislator relationships, some-thing else has helped change the way government conducts business in Tallahassee. There's more diversity in the legislative body, and it's no longer a case of power in the hands of a few.

The legislature includes more African-Americans and minorities, Collins says. And businesses that lobby before the legislative delegation now have consultants which represent that make-up. Companies are expanding their lobbying teams to include ethnic and gender diversity and philosophical diversity.

The power in the legislature has also moved from the top down, Collins says. "There was a time where you could talk to the Speaker [of the house] and talk to the President [of the senate] and they would say, 'This is what we're going to do,' and the rest would fall in line." Now, the power is among the ranks and that increases the work load.

"Issues are moving so fast, you need a small army to deal with them," he says. Residents can be assured they will be dealt with, and carried out as usual, by those ever-present, ever-employed state workers. ◆

—Julie S. Bettinger

Creating a dominant presence in Tallahassee is the New Capitol—a 22-story tower, flanked by domes. Completed in 1977, it sits only a few hundred feet behind the Old Capitol. Photo by Robert M. Overton.

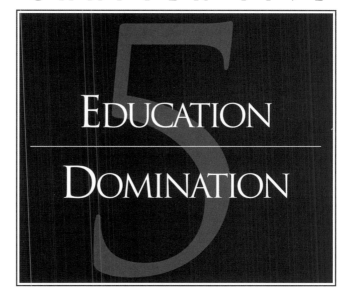

CHAPTER FIVE

EDUCATION

DOMINATION

INFLUENCING YOUNG MINDS AND LIFESTYLES

◆

"Our nation's great research universities...are defining the shape of the future. Universities are the inspiration and source of the ideas and discoveries that lead to technological progress, business and economic development, better government and laws, the creation of new art forms, and innovative ways of thinking about the destiny of the planet."

–From "The State Of Your Future," Published by Florida State University

◆

Florida State University's focus is on what it is doing for each and every individual student—building a strong foundation and providing the right tools for achievement. Photo by Robert M. Overton.

Miniature flags of garnet and gold or green and orange flap atop windows as cars cut through traffic on busy Thomasville Road. It's Saturday afternoon in Tallahassee and spirits are soaring.

Two guys wearing black wigs with beaded headbands are sporting Indian garb and red face paint. They're making rounds at Florida State University's Doak Campbell Stadium, among the crowd of 76,000 fans—many with Seminole tattoos and war-painted faces.

Not far away, under the bright lights at Bragg Stadium, everyone is under the spell of the Florida A&M University's Marching 100 Band during half time. There's revelry in the stands as the crowds move to the jazzy sounds created by trumpets, trombones, horns, and drums.

Few people are immune to Seminole Fever and Rattler Mania; it seems to grip the city. Tallahassee businesses turn tomb-like at game time, and parking becomes a premium on the southwest side of town.

These are the more obvious clues of what it's like to be living in a university town. Game day in Tallahassee is a celebration of the tradition and teaching that our universities and community college bring to this capital city.

Serving as home to two of the state's ten major state universities means more than fanfare and flags on weekends, though.

Being part of a major educational mecca also means major opportunities. At the two universities and community college, the choices are endless. Theater, music, and dance performances; distinguished guest speakers; athletic events; discussion groups; and social gatherings form an incredible range of choices for students and nonstudents alike.

And this doesn't even take into account the great gains going on inside the classroom and in the minds of our 59,000-plus students.

EDUCATION—A SERIOUS BUSINESS

Many people would agree that education is Tallahassee's major industry, as we annually export well-prepared students to destinations worldwide.

Graduates leave to follow the path of entrepreneur, executive, or manager. They lead municipal, state, and national efforts as legislators and judges. They help mold young minds as educators and administrators, counselors, and ministers. They speak to the masses as reporters and columnists; and they insure our nation's health as physicians, nurses, and pharmacists.

The FSU Seminoles compete in 16 collegiate sports and have 3 national titles, including their reign as the collegiate football national champions in 1993. Photo by Robert M. Overton.

Throughout the history of the university, music, art, and humanities have been important, and FSU is recognized for its strong cultural program. Photo by Robert M. Overton.

Through its educational institutions, Tallahassee is touching the future.

"Really our total resources in education [in Tallahassee] are unparalleled by most other locations," says James H. Hinson Jr., president of Tallahassee Community College. "There are some places that have a community college and university in the same place, but the combination of a predominantly black university, a major state university, and a community college all working as cooperatively as we do is unusual."

Fortunately for the students, he says, "We enjoy one of the best relationships that you're going to find anywhere in the country."

Tallahassee also has Lively Technical Center, one of Florida's largest training centers. Employers in the area benefit from its flexible programs which serve to supplement education and training not found at other facilities.

ROOTS AND WINGS

Then, there's Florida State University.

It would be easy to get carried away with talk of national football championships, fiscal strength, and other self-serving aspects. Instead, Talbot "Sandy" D'Alemberte, president of FSU, prefers to focus on what the university is doing for each and every individual student—building a strong foundation and providing the right tools for achievement.

"Through the history of the university—even when it was the Florida State College for Women—music, art, and humanities were important," D'Alemberte says. "And we still benefit from that."

Today FSU is recognized for having a strong cultural program. "I think that gets back to the school's roots as the Florida State College for Women," he says.

The music and theater schools rank in the top three to four in the country, according to D'Alemberte. "And the theater school has grown to be a school of great distinction. They're attracting [real talent]."

In addition, Florida State has a very strong visual arts, dance, and film school, he says.

SCIENTIFIC AND SPORTING ACHIEVEMENTS

Another dominant area, at least since the early 1950s, is the steady growth in the sciences at Florida State, D'Alemberte adds. "We have the Magnetic Lab," he points out, "a world-class scientific facility. We're all over the world now."

"We're still ranked in the top of research without a large engineering school and any medical school, which is fairly unusual. We're one of only a handful." This ranking is an indication of the high quality of research going on in the basic sciences and humanities, D'Alemberte believes.

Florida State's performance on the football field has gained wide acclaim, too, with the recent national championship title, but he adds, "We also send our baseball team on a regular basis to the college world series." The basketball program is recruiting top athletes, and he says, "Our women's softball team was among the NCA finalists and we now see [women's] basketball growing. We've got one of the most distinguished athletic programs anywhere in the country."

STUDENTS MAKE IT HAPPEN

D'Alemberte doesn't get too far away from the university's reason for being, though. That is to educate young people and prepare them for tomorrow.

"If I were to brag about anything, I would brag about the students," D'Alemberte says. "The high quality of the student body is incredible. I think we've been able to improve on our diversity; we have 25 percent minority, and 53 percent women."

And those students seem to agree that Florida State is delivering the kind of education they came for. It's an approach the faculty has worked hard to develop.

"We do a lot of surveying of students and exit interviews of [graduates]," says Elisabeth Muhlenfeld, dean of undergraduate studies. The university seeks to get the students' point of view. "There are three or four themes that keep cropping up [in the survey results], and it turns out they're exactly what we're after," Muhlenfeld says.

Diversity on campus is one aspect that students seem to enjoy, the surveys have found. "The students think it's important and recognize that the university also thinks it's important." They

Under the bright lights at Bragg Stadium, there's revelry in the stands as the crowds move to the jazzy sounds created by the Florida A&M University's Marching 100 Band. Florida A&M has long provided quality education, challenging athletic programs, and attractive facilities for its students. Photo by Robert M. Overton.

point to the diversity of origins—small towns and big towns—in addition to ethnicity and political backgrounds, according to Muhlenfeld.

"The second thing that comes up is the liberal studies and liberal arts nature of our university," Muhlenfeld says. After graduation, former students frequently cite Florida State's liberal studies and liberal arts background as important. "They seem to understand it was a good thing to get broad exposure," she says.

Unusual as it may seem, the most popular majors are not business, as many people assume. The order is criminology, biological sciences, English, psychology, political science, and communication. Number seven is accounting, the first business-related major in the list. "For a large public university that's very unusual," Muhlenfeld says.

In addition, she says, "Students are proud of the fact that we have a high caliber of cultural activities on campus. They're more culturally aware and support the fine arts. We've built that into our liberal studies program."

ATHLETICS STILL CAPABLE OF A DEAFENING ROAR

Graduating students continue to give their support to the university through the Seminole Booster Club, Alumni Association, and education-related endowments. And they are rewarded by seeing their school in the spotlight, whether it be for scientific or athletic achievements.

Lawton Langford, chairman of the Seminole Boosters, Inc., says, "The credit for our national reputation really does go to football." Pointing to a recent *New York Times* feature article discussing the Mag Lab versus Massachusetts Institute of Technology, Langford says, "Bobby Bowden's name was in the first paragraph—why else but because winning football has gained us national recognition?"

Langford says no one can discount the role athletics plays in this attraction of students. "It helps in promotion and marketing of the school," he says.

Florida State is able to retain support year after year, according to Langford. No booster program in the country raises more money and has more people supporting it than Florida State's. FSU has even passed Clemson, the perennial leader, he says.

Booster funds go beyond athletics, though. In fact, the Seminole Boosters are guaranteeing the repaying of the bond on the University Center, a $96-million project which has added 500,000 square feet of classroom space and administrative offices.

Langford credits Andy Miller, president of the boosters, for the idea, but it was a coalition of faculty, students, administration, and state legislators who pulled it off. "And that's what has made it successful," he says.

ECONOMIC POWERHOUSE

Florida A&M University has long provided quality education, challenging athletic programs, and attractive facilities for its students, but under the leadership of President Frederick S. Humphries, it now stands on the brink of becoming a major economic powerhouse.

FAMU is the third oldest institution in the State University System of Florida, and few people are as proud of the Rattlers as Humphries.

A giant of a man, Humphries charms students, faculty, and audiences with his eloquence and broad smile. A native of Apalachicola, Humphries graduated magna cum laude from FAMU in 1957 with a bachelor's in chemistry. He went on to earn his Ph.D. degree in physical chemistry at the University of Pittsburgh in 1964. He took over the helm at FAMU in 1985.

"Several years ago, we made a commitment to attract National Achievement Scholars [NAS]—the very best [academically talented] black students graduating from high school in any given year," Humphries says.

In 1992 FAMU was number one in the nation for NAS recruitment. It was the first time a historically black college or university defeated Harvard for the nation's top black students, he notes. He credits the foundation they've built along the way for positioning the school for the top spot.

"It has been easy to attract those students—one, because FAMU has a good academic program, and two, the top kids are normally interested in the [fields of study] we offer."

Then there's the campus itself, which sits on top of one of Tallahassee's highest hills. Stately buildings, many of which have been newly renovated, evoke pride in alumni and other visitors as they walk among the giant oaks and grassy knolls. "I think the campus, the programs, and the city itself have helped us be [more attractive] to the very best students," Humphries says.

EDUCATION CONTINUES BEYOND FAMU

In addition to a pleasant experience while they're here, Humphries wants to assure a promising future for graduates of Florida A&M—and part of that plan includes encouragement for pursuing further education.

He helped establish the Graduate Feeder Program in order to boost the number of minorities attending graduate school. "We determined there was an under representation of African-American students in graduate programs," he says. "We decided if we could form an alliance with graduate schools and deliver students to them, it would be helpful to our students and [the schools]."

Through the Graduate Feeder Program, each institution has agreed to reserve three to five admission slots for qualified FAMU graduates. These students have the opportunity to pursue graduate and professional degrees not offered by Florida A&M University. Feeder institutions provide tuition, room and board, application fee waivers, book stipends, and assistantships/ fellowships to qualified applicants.

Since the establishment of the Graduate Feeder Program, Humphries says FAMU has become a major player in sending African-American students to graduate and professional schools. "We started with 15 schools, and we're now at 28," Humphries says. About 150 students go straight to graduate programs annually.

THE BIG MONEY GAME

Humphries' strategy of building a world-renowned institution of higher learning includes attracting dollars for research, academics, and scholarships. "The basic thrust of raising the dollars is to permit the university to have scholarship dollars to attract the best and brightest to the university and to have the kind of faculty that can excite those students and give them a much broader vision," he says. "We want the teachers who are best in their field."

The university's research was the first area of concentration. "We're now in the number one position in attraction of research dollars among historically black colleges. And we're fourth or fifth among the state universities. We're proud of that."

But dollars and research don't always mean results, Humphries admits. By emphasizing technology transfer, he says, FAMU is assured of a longer lasting outcome.

"We're certainly looking for the end results," he says. "We're looking for potential applications. We want to assure that the work of our researchers ultimately winds up creating jobs."

A COMMUNITY LEADER

James Hinson, president of Tallahassee Community College, is big on the working relationship established between FSU, FAMU, TCC, and Lively Technical Center.

Tallahassee Community College has a reputation for high quality instruction and maintaining a close relationship with universities for the purpose of student transferal. Photo by Robert M. Overton.

The person most likely to benefit, of course, is the student transferring from one institution to another. "We have a reputation for high quality instruction and maintaining a close relationship with universities for the purpose of transferring," Hinson says. He attributes the nearly "seamless transition" to planning with university administrators.

Hinson also takes the role of the community college in our tapestry of educational offerings seriously. "I tell people the greatest bargain in higher education is the community college," Hinson says. "The fee level is still relatively low. Students pay only about $1,000 a year in student fees to attend TCC. That's a remarkable value. For that $1,000, you get an extremely high value of educational services."

The community college has an obligation to be fiscally conservative, and he says TCC allocates its resources to instruction at a much higher rate than any other community college in the country. "In [the 1993-1994 school year], 57 percent of our budget went directly to the classroom," he says. That's compared to a 51 percent state average.

"We also have the lowest administrative cost of any community college in the state," he says. The state's support cost average is $320 per student higher than the cost of TCC. "There's very little in the way of bureaucracy here," he says. "We make decisions easier and faster."

Hinson adds that even though they've gained a reputation of being fiscally responsible, the school has been able to retain the best teachers. And that makes it even more attractive with fall 1994 enrollment reaching 10,300.

"We have the most qualified faculty of any community college in the state," Hinson says. "One of the highest in the nation," he says. "By virtue of any objective measure you put to it—years of experience, number of Ph.D. degrees, faculty preparation—TCC leads the state in those measures."

"That happens not by accident," he continues. "It happens by design. The design is to allocate our resources so we pay the highest—and we do. We have the highest average salary [among the 28 community colleges] in the state of Florida by considerable margins."

The result has been a big savings in faculty retention. Upon his retirement in June 1995, Hinson says, "I will have 12 years of never having lost a faculty member to another college. We may have lost them to promotion or retirement, but not to another institution. And that's absolutely remarkable."

Student performance—measured after they have left TCC—helps illustrate Hinson's points.

"The educational outcomes of our students validate our claims for having the high quality education services," he says. "To give examples of that, when we transfer students to universities, they tend to make the same grade point average as the junior year class that they are joining. They tend to maintain the same [grade point average] or higher than they earned at TCC. Both of those measures are indexes to a quality education."

And for those who don't go on to other institutions, such as those in the occupational programs—including nursing, dental hygiene, and emergency medical technician—he says the school maintains a 100 percent placement rate in the job market. "We've not gone below 90 percent—even in the recession," he says.

TCC has attracted a significant amount of campus improvement funds from the state to acquire land, according to Hinson. The campus has grown from 65 acres to nearly 200 acres. "We don't intend to become landlocked," he says. "And that's part of our master plan."

Another part of the master plan is to expand TCC's athletic program. Only three years old, he says the women's softball team has already gained a national championship, and all three teams—baseball, basketball, and softball—went to state championship play-offs.

There's a renewed commitment to wellness, with the start of a fitness center which is available to students, faculty, and staff. It's located in the "Lifetime Sports Complex."

Facilities like the fitness center are examples of the types of resources available to Tallahasseeans—all because of our educational institutions.

THE HIGHER EDUCATION/PUBLIC SCHOOL BRIDGE

Higher education resources in Tallahassee also manage to make a distinct imprint on Leon County public schools. After all, someone's got to mold those little Seminole and Rattler minds.

In his prediction about education in the year 2009 published in *Tallahassee* magazine, Richard Merrick, superintendent of Leon County schools, described several changes that have taken root to shape our children and future.

"The first area I see a lot of changes in is instructional strategies," Merrick said. "I think what you will see is a teacher being less of a performer and more of a leader and coach, and the emphasis is going to be on student work. The student's role will be that of a hands-on performer more than a listener."

The hands-on approach is something Kathy Safford, sixth grade science teacher at Cobb Middle School, is working to introduce to the 157 students she sees daily.

On a characteristically warm fall morning in her science lab, Safford was introducing a lesson:

"We're going to do what I call Cupcake Geology today," Safford announced. She asked student helpers to distribute one cupcake per student, along with a clear plastic straw and knife.

"The cupcake represents the earth's core," she told the class. The 20 or so students were to pretend they were scientists, observe and draw the cupcake, then use the straw to drill into it at different angles, labeling each core sample taken. They were to hypothesize about the layers of the cupcake—most of which had multiple colors and candies melted into them. The 12-year-olds were learning how to research through hands-on application.

After hypothesizing, the students were to slice the cupcake in half to see how accurate they had been. The samples were eventually consumed—a reward for the patient scientists.

A teacher for 21 years, Safford is also seeking to build a bridge between university resources and the public schools. She annually takes her students on a field trip to Florida State University. Half of the students attend a lecture hall where Penny Gilmer, a physics professor, gives her "Mrs. Wizard" chemistry-physics magic show. The other half is given a tour of the planetarium by Gerald Hart, another professor.

That's another prediction by Merrick for the year 2009: "There will be at all levels—especially at high school levels—a much closer collaboration between the public schools and the community colleges and universities."

As Tallahassee's rich educational heritage continues to engage young minds, it's likely be demonstrated by more than Seminole heads on clothing and green and orange ribbons intertwined with braids. ◆

—Julie S. Bettinger

Higher education resources in Tallahassee make a distinct imprint on Leon County public schools. Through its quality educational institutions, Tallahassee is touching the future. Photo by Robert M. Overton.

C H A P T E R   S I X

PORTRAIT OF
OUR PEOPLE

PERSPECTIVES AND
PERSONALITIES

◆

*"Once upon a time, Tallahassee
was a small town, and everybody
thought they were the same, even
though that obviously wasn't true.
Now, with the city changing, our
differences are apparent but we
can still take advantage of that
small-town feel by celebrating
the diversity of the city."*

–Dave Fiore,
Editor of *Tallahassee* Magazine

◆

*"The sweetness of life, I think, comes from the love of your family and the
love of the Lord," says Arthur J. Burns, a third generation Tallahasseean
who, as a boy, flew in the city's first privately owned airplane. "I've worked
all my life—farming, building houses, breaking oxen, working for the WPA,
welding, bulldozing, roofing, butchering hogs and cows, working as a
mechanic, and spending time in the service, and I've never had money. But
my, how my life has been full and blessed and rich. I just try to live by the
Bible, treat people the way I want to be treated, and take care of land the
way God meant it to be cared for." Photo by Robert M. Overton.*

When George Koikos, owner of the Spartan Restaurant, makes a delicious pot of seafood gumbo, he prepares a rich fish stock, stirs in a generous amount of pungent roux, throws in a variety of fresh seafood, and then adds several handfuls of coarsely chopped vegetables. These soon simmer into a thick, chunky base, but the real secret to a delectable gumbo, he says, is in the spices.

Likewise is the creation of a city such as Tallahassee. Healthy portions of environment, private businesses, educational institutions, and state government provide a stable foundation for building a community, but it's the people—the spice—that transform an otherwise average urban area into a charming Southern town full of passion and personality.

Being home to state government, hundreds of statewide associations, and several institutions of higher learning, Tallahassee attracts an interesting blend of professions and personalities. Statistically, 40 percent of Leon County's

Calvin Jones calls himself a dirt digger, an archaeologist who looks to the ground for insight into the past instead of relying on theories and computer analyses. The reason? "Dirt don't lie," he says. Photo by Robert M. Overton.

"Tallahassee is one of the best—if not the best—places for children in the state of Florida, and I know Florida," remarks Jack Levine. As executive director of the Florida Center for Children and Youth, Levine spreads the message that healthy children and strong families are essential to a bright future. Photo by Robert M. Overton.

210,000 residents are between the ages of 25 and 49, with a median age of 29.

Descriptively, these people represent a rainbow of occupations and viewpoints. There are technicians, beauticians, massage therapists, political analysts, philosophers, intellects, teachers, preachers, and poets, to name a few. Such a strange and wonderful mix of talents and resources strengthens the community as a whole and gives it a unique flavor—an identity unlike any other city in Florida.

CALVIN JONES

Calvin Jones calls himself a dirt digger, an archaeologist who looks to the ground for insight into the past instead of relying on theories and computer analyses. The reason? "Dirt don't lie," he says. "Unfortunately, there is so little accurate knowledge of the people who came before us. Digging provides hard evidence, allowing us to learn the truth and eliminate the hype."

Jones can't remember a time when he wasn't digging. His first find—an arrowhead—fueled his desire to learn more about his Indian heritage, and by high school, he was skipping school every Friday to excavate a nearby Caddoan site. Even though journalists from *Life* magazine accompanied Jones for 10 days on one of his excavations, his principal failed to recognize its importance and repeatedly paddled Jones each Monday for skipping school on Friday. Undeterred, Jones continued his interest in archaeology and has spent his life stumbling upon pieces of the past.

Although Jones has uncovered a number of spectacular sites throughout his career, his most important historic find is the 1987 discovery of the Tallahassee de Soto site, the oldest known European campsite in the United States and the beginning of United States culture as we know it today. Pieces of brass chain mail, coins, pig bones, and pottery shards date the site to 1539, 100 years earlier than he had previously estimated.

Despite significant finds such as these, Jones regards his profession as a privilege, a luxury in a society facing so many problems. "Immediate needs come first, but then, maybe our work can help us learn more about live human beings. So much living came before us, and while we can't correct the injustices of the past, we can learn what happened and try not to repeat history."

JACK LEVINE

"Tallahassee is one of the best—if not the best—places for children in the state of Florida, and I know Florida," remarks Jack Levine. He's not kidding. As executive director of the Florida Center for Children and Youth, Levine frequently zig-zags across the state's 67 counties, spreading the message that healthy children and strong families are essential to a bright future.

Levine's former career as a teacher afforded him the opportunity to work daily with children, but he found himself outraged by the challenges they faced and frustrated that there was only so much a teacher could do. In his current position, which he has held for 15 years, he is able to intervene on behalf of those with no vote and no voice by helping shape the policies and laws affecting kids.

Ironically, the drawback to being a spokesman for the needs of children and families is the time he spends away from his own wife and two boys. "They sacrifice a lot," Levine says, "but as the boys get older, they're proud of me for being out there for kids who don't have what they do."

And as for Tallahassee, Levine gives the city good marks for the low stress level of everyday life and because of the parental involvement in area schools. Still, he emphasizes there is work to be done in improving the lives of its children. "The bottom line is that we are a community, and children aren't separate entities. What we want for our own children is what we should want for other children."

ERNEST FERRELL

There is a fine line between Ernest Ferrell's calling as pastor of Saint Mary's Primitive Baptist Church and his career as president and CEO of the Tallahassee Urban League. "It's a perfect mix for me, because I can preach on Sunday and then practice what I preach Monday through Saturday," he says. "Besides, it's really all about the same thing—helping people who can't help themselves."

Dressed in a dapper three-piece suit—his usual attire—Ferrell leans across the stacks of papers and files piled haphazardly on his desk and admits that it's no easy task. "It can be frustrating. Many times, I'll tell our story, but I know that people aren't listening to what I have to say. Plus, there's no guarantee that our doors will be open tomorrow. Getting funding is one thing, but keeping it is another." Despite these obstacles, Ferrell's success rate for program implementation is high, with over 50 programs currently offered that last from one to 15 years.

In the end, Ferrell has found that the rewards far outweigh the costs, even if it sometimes takes five years to see results in the lives of people who turn to the Urban League for help. "There's nothing like seeing a person's face light up when he realizes there is someone to help him out of a dilemma," he comments.

There is a fine line between Ernest Ferrell's calling as pastor of Saint Mary's Primitive Baptist Church and his career as president and CEO of the Tallahassee Urban League. "It's a perfect mix for me, because I can preach on Sunday and then practice what I preach Monday through Saturday," he says. Photo by Robert M. Overton.

Jack Buford Jr. has spent his life working to help Tallahassee grow gracefully into the twenty-first century. "What I try to do is promote development that broadens the economic base without jeopardizing the environmental assets we've been blessed with," Buford says. Photo by Robert M. Overton.

"If I'm in the position to help someone pull himself up, I'm willing to give what I have to make a difference."

JACK BUFORD JR.

A fourth generation Tallahasseean, Jack Buford Jr. has spent his life working to help the city grow gracefully into the twenty-first century. Each line on his lengthy résumé confirms his commitment: state government work, real estate brokering, directing an investments company, service on an assortment of community committees and boards of directors, and finally, his current role as co-owner of Tallahassee Land Company, a local business that transforms raw land into suitable space for development.

Jack's vision for Tallahassee is simple: broaden the economic base while retaining the city's high quality of life. "I like Tallahassee the way it was when I grew up here in the 1950s," he says. "But it's unrealistic to think that it won't grow. What I try to do is promote development that broadens the economic base without jeopardizing the environmental assets we've been blessed with."

ANN BIDLINGMAIER

In 1981 Ann Bidlingmaier became a local celebrity by putting herself between a bulldozer and a live oak that was about to be uprooted. Her stance sparked a controversy that continues today: nurture and protect Tallahassee's natural environment or develop the land to promote area growth.

As a young school teacher, Bidlingmaier never intended to become a tree vigilante. In fact, she still doesn't consider

herself a tree hugger. "Tree huggers are nerds," she says. "I'd rather be a healing force, someone who bridges the gap between both sides. Most people don't realize, though, that in order to do so, you sometimes have to light a few fires."

Today, Bidlingmaier continues her crusade by educating people about the importance of trees. "It sounds simplistic, but trees are healthy for everyone in the community," she explains. "They also act like big sponges, soaking up storm water and preventing erosion."

People who can't see the forest for the trees is perhaps Bidlingmaier's biggest beef. "My goal is to see a Tallahassee 20 years down the road that hasn't been assaulted and polluted by short visions," she says. "Instead of developing green spaces, why not revitalize existing shopping malls and industrial sites?"

A native of Broward County, Bidlingmaier moved to and stayed in Tallahassee because of its natural beauty, and though her father was involved in development when she was growing up, she says he is proud of her efforts in Tallahassee. "My dad is supportive of my work because he has seen what has happened in his hometown. They once had trees like us; he just never realized how far it would go."

And what happened to the live oak that she saved? It's the lone tree on a lot that has remained mostly undeveloped since its grazing 13 years ago.

THE SPRINGFIELD SEVEN

"Up with hope! Down with dope! Walk a mile; save a child! What time is it? It's drug fighting time!" On any given day, a small parade of seven women dressed in matching T-shirts and hard hats can be found marching up and down the streets of the Springfield Apartment Complex off Joe Louis Street. Their message? Drugs destroy lives. Their mission? To drive drug dealers and related crime out of their neighborhood.

And it's working, thanks to the efforts of the Springfield Seven: Julia Bell, Beneka Ceasor, Rose M. Hall, Darlene Maddox, Mary Mosley, Tamika Perryman, and Marilyn Turner.

The women created Springfield Neighbors Against Drugs (SNAD) in February 1993, after they participated in a seminar

Ann Bidlingmaier never intended to become a tree vigilante and she doesn't consider herself a tree hugger. "Tree huggers are nerds," she says. "I'd rather be a healing force, someone who bridges the gap between both sides." Photo by Robert M. Overton.

Due to the visibility and determination of the Springfield Seven, their children can play outside without fear of gunfire and altercations—something unheard of only two years ago. "Instead of moving, we simply changed our neighborhood," remarks Beneka Ceasor. Photo by Robert M. Overton.

sponsored by the United States Justice Department's Weed and Seed Program, a grassroots campaign aimed at identifying and eliminating drug dealers from neighborhoods. "In our first parade, hundreds of people marched with us," recalls Perryman. Because of her past experiences, she now leads outreach support meetings in her home for others who are trying to get their lives together. "We had city and county commissioners, representatives from the Justice Department, and even drug dealers wearing our T-shirts and marching up and down the streets."

Now, most marches usually consist of only the seven and their children, but due to their visibility and determination, their children can play outside without fear of gunfire and altercations—something unheard of only two years ago. The seven also have the support and encouragement of TPD Officer Alan Smith and Sergeant Maurice Laws, who quickly respond to any reports of drug-related activity in the neighborhood. Their efforts were noticed by Chief Thomas Coe, who nominated the group for Civic Volunteer of the Year, an award they won in 1994.

There are other side effects of SNAD. "It has made us stand up and fight for ourselves in other ways," confides Hall, a mother of two. "It was a life-changing experience."

Turner, who has five children, including newborn twins, agrees. "I want my kids to look up to me instead of Michael Jordan. That's one reason I'm going back to college. I need to get higher so I can help them get higher."

So sure of their mission, these women never looked back—only ahead—at what they might accomplish. "You have a right to fight for your community, and it doesn't take a hundred people to make a difference," remarks Ceasor. "Instead of moving, we simply changed our neighborhood."

PAM LAWS

In 1986 jazz singer Pam Laws traveled to the Soviet Union as part of a delegation sent to represent Tallahassee in its sister city, Krasnodar. It was a turning point in her career. "These people were supposedly the enemy, yet they were so warm and giving," remembers Laws. "I had completely overlooked the meaning of what I was doing, and it was then that I realized that singing wasn't just about entertaining."

As a child, Laws was exposed to a variety of arts by her parents, who were FAMU professors. One field—music—particularly interested her, and soon her father had bought her a little yellow record player with an assortment of records to entertain her. "At first, there were kiddy records, but these were slowly replaced by Chopin, piano concertos, and Mozart," she says. "I would spend most nights sitting in bed, reading and listening to music on my record player or on the radio. I was practically raised on it."

Later, Laws majored in music at FAMU and continued to foster her love by pursuing a master's degree in opera at Indiana University. But the music wasn't in her soul. "My parents wanted me to study opera, but it was 1968, and I was stuck in the midwest singing some opera on a stage in a German woman's clothing. I just had to get out of there." To escape, she joined the American Red Cross, leaving Indiana just before earning her master's degree.

Today, Laws spends her days teaching English and jazz history at Tallahassee Community College. At night, she can often be found on the Tallahassee night scene, howling the blues of Dinah Washington or cooing to her audience with lullabies and traditional gospel tunes.

For Laws, music has always been easy. "It feels like a woman sent up a song millions of years ago and all I have to do is reach up and latch on." But she also insists that her musical career is successful in part because of the local support and encouragement she receives. "People are so kind to me, and willing to pass my name along. I think that I could have done what I do here in another city, but you would never have heard of me."

MICHAEL DAVIDSON

Dressed in blue jeans, a T-shirt, and sneakers, and sporting a neatly trimmed haircut and well-groomed mustache, Michael Davidson doesn't look the part of a mad scientist, much less a fashion designer. But he is both—and neither—at the same time, in dual careers that are surprisingly parallel.

Davidson, a senior research engineer at the National High Magnetic Field Laboratory at FSU, has spent most of his life

studying liquid crystals and DNA. Curious about how DNA forms, Davidson began photographing the chromosomes under polarized light through an optical microscope, a process known as photomicrography. It was there that he discovered his second career. "I started seeing these really beautiful patterns and photographing them," he recalls. "So from there I began photographing other things just because I was interested."

In 1988 Davidson's work in both fields was recognized: his research—along with a brilliant photomicrograph on the cover—was published in *Nature,* a prestigious British scientific journal; and one of his photographs won the photomicrography division of the Polaroid Corporation's international photo competition, an award he would capture again in 1991. Soon after, a colleague suggested he contact manufacturers to see if they were interested in reproducing his images on fabric.

Today, Davidson's photomicrographs of vitamins, mixed drinks, and even candy can be found on a number of items ranging from dance and aerobic wear to T-shirts and ties to ladies' accessories and scarves. He has even designed a line of bedding accessories. With each purchase, a portion of the proceeds goes to the Mag Lab, where Davidson is currently working with high-tech materials such as superconductors and semiconductors.

And there is a method to his madness. "They complement each other," he says of his two careers. "What I hope to do is capture children's and adults' attention with a photograph and then feed them a little science along with it." ◆

—Heidi Tyline King

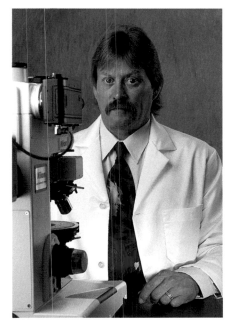

Shown wearing his own creation—a Vitamin B tie—Michael Davidson is a senior research engineer at the National High Magnetic Field Laboratory at FSU. "What I hope to do is capture children's and adults' attention with a photograph and then feed them a little science along with it," comments Davidson. Photo courtesy of Florida State University.

CHAPTER SEVEN

A City Of Arts, Festivals, & Natural Attractions

What's Left Of The Old Florida

◆

"We're not New York, and we don't want to be New York. Yet even though we look like a small town, we have some very interesting things to do here. It's just a matter of getting out and enjoying Tallahassee and what it has to offer."

–Melanie Annis,
Publisher of *Q Magazine*

◆

Antebellum mansions throughout the area are an example of Tallahassee's charm. Photo by Robert M. Overton.

There's something rather odd about seeing *Tallahassee* emblazoned across the front of a touristy T-shirt. Unlike her neon neighbors, the city has no avenues lined with souvenir shops, no crowded theme parks and galleries; there's not even a mascot or a mouse.

What visitors will find is an unexpected side of Florida: a side as unusual—and as endangered—as the state's manatees. Often described as "what's left of the old Florida," Tallahassee is literally a curtain of green. Instead of imposing, high-rise hotels, patriarch oaks jut above the sun-dappled skyline. On a basic road map, the scattering of verdant parks and the assortment of recreational lakes and rivers command as much attention as the state roads and interstate highways. And because of the city's subtropical climate, both native and exotic shrubs and flowers often give an encore following their spring performance.

Memories are made here, attractions are of a different kind, and amusements are found in places other than parks. These are the perennial souvenirs that you'll pack away in the pockets of your mind after a trip to Tallahassee. Besides, the only thing a tourist can gain from a T-shirt is finding out that *Tallahassee* is harder to spell than M-I-S-S-I-S-S-I-P-P-I!

THE TALLAHASSEE SYMPHONY ORCHESTRA

The Tallahassee Symphony Orchestra, founded in 1979 by Nicholas Harsanyi, is a professional symphony orchestra that performs symphonic and classical music in concert and chamber settings. Under the direction of David Hoose, the symphony is

LeMoyne Art Foundation is the city's oldest art gallery. Both permanent and traveling exhibits by local, regional, and national visual artists are routinely featured in the gallery. Photo by Robert M. Overton.

LuElla Knott's carefully restored home depicts life as it existed in the 1930s. Author, poet, and musician, Miss Knott was so inspired by her collection of Victorian furnishings that she wrote poems about each piece and attached them to the furniture with satin ribbons. Photo by Robert M. Overton.

made up of 100 artists, including music faculty from FSU and FAMU, professional musicians from the Tallahassee community, and talented students from area colleges.

Because tickets to symphony performances have been sold out for the past four years, plans are currently underway to expand the concert series by providing double performances to the community.

TALLAHASSEE BALLET

Now in its 22nd season, the Tallahassee Ballet has grown from a small regional ballet to a strong, semi-professional company featuring local, regional, and national professional guest artists. Founded by Helen Salter, this non-profit organization strives to provide the community with exceptional productions of classical and contemporary works. The company also works to stimulate interest and appreciation for the dance arts in the north Florida area, and provides local dancers and emerging professionals with a professional training ground.

BLACK ARCHIVES RESEARCH CENTER AND MUSEUM

The Black Archives Research Center and Museum is one of the most extensive archives and artifacts collections of African-American history in the Southeast. While many other museums of its kind are now popping up throughout the country, this established research facility has been in existence almost 30 years.

According to archivist Murrell Dawson, the museum provides visitors with a first-hand look at the lives and experiences of African-Americans and people of color throughout the world. "Our motto is 'Afro-American history is the history of America,'" says Dawson. The archives and museum give testimony to these contributions.

LEMOYNE ART FOUNDATION

Incorporated in 1963, LeMoyne Art Foundation is the city's oldest art gallery. Both permanent and traveling exhibits by local, regional, and national visual artists are routinely featured in the gallery. In addition, the magnificent gardens laid out in the back of the gallery offer an elegant backdrop for the sculpture displayed on the grounds and the art openings sponsored by the museum.

The Black Archives Research Center and Museum provides visitors with a first-hand look at the lives and experiences of African-Americans and people of color throughout the world. Photo by Robert M. Overton.

LeMoyne is a supporter of community arts and offers a variety of classes and workshops on various art topics for both adults and children throughout the year. Since 1968 LeMoyne has been housed in the historic Meginniss-Munroe antebellum home.

KNOTT HOUSE MUSEUM

"I'm just an old, old home, And you are welcome here; Listen and look, and find in me Spirit and atmosphere."

There's more rhyme and reason to this museum than just a display of fine antiques and turn-of-the-century memorabilia. Rather, this carefully restored home depicts life as it existed in the 1930s, from the yellowed pieces of mail and vintage magazines scattered on top of Mr. Knott's desk to the hand-cut and pieced French wallpaper flanking the stairs.

Yet perhaps the most important piece of history preserved is the memory of the eccentric personality of the home's last mistress, LuElla Knott. An author, poet, and musician, LuElla was so inspired by her unique collection of Victorian furnishings that she wrote poems about each piece and attached them to the furniture with satin ribbons. Full of clever wit and an occasional moral, these poems earned the Knott House its nickname, "the house that rhymed."

MUSEUM OF FLORIDA HISTORY

This State of Florida museum is one of the perks to being a capital city. With exhibits ranging from the prehistoric to the present, the museum is a visual time line of the people and events that shaped the sunshine state.

Buckskin clothing embellished with elaborate beadwork and 14-foot canoes, each carved from a single tree, offer visitors a glimpse of the lifestyles of Florida's first inhabitants, the Indians. Treasures from old Spanish galleons provide insight to the explorers who tried to claim Florida as their own. Pioneer homesteads resembling those described by Marjorie Kinnan Rawlings exemplify the simplicity and hardship of pioneer life. And above it all, a nine-foot skeleton, assembled from bones cast from a mastodon discovered at nearby Wakulla Springs, serves as a towering reminder of Florida's earliest days. Permanent exhibits such as these are enhanced by traveling tours, special events, and educational programs that frequently feature Florida's various cultures and environments.

FLORIDA STATE CAPITOL—BOTH OLD AND NEW

A reverence for history and a hope for the future; a contrast between the "old" and "new" Florida; a push for progress in territories paved by the past. Perched atop one of Tallahassee's highest hills, the close proximity of the Old and the New Capitol is one of the best examples of how the past and the present can complement each other.

The New Capitol was completed in 1977, and from its 22nd floor, one can see all the way to the Gulf Coast on a clear day. The governor's office is on the plaza level; the secretary of state, members of the governor's cabinet, and legislative offices are also housed in the building. It sits only a few hundred feet behind the Old Capitol because original plans called for the old building be to destroyed.

Today, the Old Capitol is part of the Museum of Florida History, and offers exhibits on the state's political and social development.

TALLAHASSEE-LEON COUNTY CIVIC CENTER

"There's no event that we can't handle," says Ron Spencer, director of the Tallahassee-Leon County Civic Center. From the wide variety of entertainment available to Tallahasseeans via the civic center, no one is arguing. Popular contemporary artists reach a large regional population segment by performing here; country artists like Tallahassee because of its small-town feel. Alternative and reggae musicians are attracted to the large student population.

With one of the nation's only two theatrical grid systems designed exclusively for use outside of performing arts centers, the civic center annually draws touring Broadway series. And with tremendous support from the community, Tallahassee is now home to the Tiger Sharks, the newest hockey team in the East Coast Hockey League.

SPRINGTIME TALLAHASSEE

Moving a state capital seems almost ludicrous in today's technologically advanced world, but as recently as 1968, there was talk about relocating the seat of Florida's government to a more centralized location. To counter such chatter, Tallahasseean Betty McCord set out to promote the city's rich heritage and high quality of life to the rest of the state. Her answer? Springtime Tallahassee.

Perhaps no other city in the South can boast such a spectacular display of spring than the capital city. And certainly no other city can match Tallahassee's contributions to shaping the state of Florida. The festival has now blossomed into a four-week jubilee in celebration of spring and Florida history, and is considered by some to be the city's premier event of the year. Several events held throughout the city lead up to the main day of celebration, which literally overflows into the streets of downtown Tallahassee.

SAN LUIS HERITAGE FESTIVAL

Historic reenactments, traditional foods, and music are part of the San Luis festivities in honor of Florida's cultural heritage. The site of this festival, which features a seventeenth-century Spanish mission and Indian settlement created some 200 years before Florida became a state, is only one of many archaeological "gems" discovered in the Tallahassee area.

HARAMBE FESTIVAL

A celebration of African-American culture, the Harambe Festival is a holistic experience of the sights, sounds, and expressions that compose the African-American lifestyle. Local, regional, and national performing, visual, and folk artists provide exhibits, presentations, and performances during the weekend event that culminates Black History month. In addition to the versatility of performances and the variety of booths, there is a black film festival, a museum displaying African artifacts, a forum for the exchange of ideas and issues concerning black artists, and a Harambe Exchange, which is a brain bowl competition for middle and secondary students on black history.

CELEBRATE AMERICA

Patriotism is popping, literally, at this annual fireworks display at Tom Brown Park. The largest of its kind in the area, the festival also includes sporting events and patriotic performances for the 50,000 attendees.

THE WINTER FESTIVAL: A CELEBRATION OF LIGHTS, MUSIC, AND THE ARTS

In 1987 city planners purchased about $70,000 in new holiday decorations. Little did they know that a wildly popular winter festival would be one of the results of their purchases. That first year, a small, one-night event in honor of lighting the new decorations was planned to kick off the holiday season. Over 6,000 people showed up, and the numbers—and activities—have grown ever since.

Today, the Winter Festival is a two-week celebration featuring family programs, a holiday music and fine arts competition, outdoor ice skating, and cultural arts entertainment. Santa's Enchanted Forest, which is really a city park transformed into a winter wonderland by city staff, is one of the event's most popular attractions. The lighting of the decorations, however, remains the centerpiece of the festival.

CITY PARKS AND RECREATION SERVICES

Whether sunshine or shade, Tallahassee is paradise for the avid sportsman. In the local vicinity alone, there are more than 60 bowling lanes, 72-plus holes of golf, and more than 1,800 acres in the 55 public parks for tennis, racquetball, picnicking, basketball, baseball, and walking.

Not only are the area's parks enjoyed by the locals, but they're also a drawing card in attracting sports events to the capital city. The abundant parks, as well as athletic facilities at local universities, also contributed to the decision made by the British

Perhaps no other city in the South can boast such a spectacular display of spring than the capital city. Springtime Tallahassee has now blossomed into a four-week jubilee in celebration of the season and Florida history. Photo courtesy of Springtime Tallahassee Committee.

Olympic Association to use Tallahassee as the training site for the 1996 Olympic Games in Atlanta. At this writing, Tallahassee is the only city to host an entire country's Olympic delegation. Tallahassee will also serve as the British headquarters during the Olympics.

Dedicated on Veteran's Day 1985, Florida's Vietnam Era Veterans' Memorial honors the state's known Vietnam casualties and soldiers missing in action. Each of these soldiers' names is inscribed in the monument's black marble. Photo by Robert M. Overton.

HUNTING AND FISHING

Because the temperature averages 50 degrees in the winter and 83 degrees in the summer, Tallahassee is also host to other outdoor activities such as cycling and hiking. For cycling enthusiasts, the shaded canopy roads are perfect escapes for pedaling pleasures. Hikers find that the city and nearby state parks provide excellent trails, such as the Florida National Scenic Trail, which is the only United States trail out of eight that remains hikeable during the winter.

Fishing and boating on the numerous lakes and rivers surrounding the city are also pleasurable pastimes. In fact, the fishing is so good that people come to Tallahassee from all over the country just to fish.

Another sporting delight is hunting, which is so popular that many of the nineteenth-century "gentleman" plantations surrounding the city were transformed into hunting lodges by wealthy winter residents. Quail, turkey, duck, geese, squirrels,

and white-tail deer are among the wildlife that send hunters trekking to area forests and hunt clubs.

TALLAHASSEE MUSEUM OF HISTORY AND NATURAL SCIENCE

The Tallahassee Museum of History and Natural Science is more than just a zoo. By combining native wildlife and early vernacular architecture in an unspoiled natural setting, the museum attempts to preserve endangered pieces of our region's cultural and natural heritage from a common predator: progress. Birds and animals injured and unable to survive in the wild can find a home at the museum, while the museum's endangered animals, the Florida panthers and the red wolves, are participants in state and federal breeding and repopulation programs.

In addition to the animal habitats, historical buildings are rescued from destruction and brought to the museum's grounds for restoration.

Founded in 1957, the museum exemplifies the intricate relationship that exists between people and their environment. Traditional woodworking, quilting and sewing, syrup-making, and farming are a few of the on-going living history programs that attract more than 125,000 annual visitors.

GOVERNOR'S MANSION

If it weren't for the massive wrought-iron fence surrounding the property, no one would guess that the Florida governor's mansion lies nestled behind the shady magnolias on the grounds. Built in 1956, the Georgian-style Southern mansion features a portico designed similarly to that of Andrew Jackson's columned home, the Hermitage. Inside, the home is furnished with eighteenth- and nineteenth-century collectibles, with state rooms displaying gifts from foreign dignitaries. And because it is located only one mile from the Capitol, the governor could easily walk to and from his office.

DE SOTO STATE HISTORIC SITE

Before the discovery of this historic site, archaeologists and historians could only speculate about the location of de Soto's encampment during his first winter in Florida. When physical evidence was uncovered, the proof was overwhelming. Among the 40,000 artifacts recovered were Spanish and Indian pottery dating to the 1500s, glass trade beads, links of chain mail armor, coins from the early 1500s, and the jaw of a pig, which was unknown to the New World.

Presently, the site is the only confirmed de Soto camp in North America, and it is ironically located less than a mile from the Capitol.

FLORIDA'S VIETNAM ERA VETERANS' MEMORIAL

Dedicated on Veteran's Day 1985, Florida's Vietnam Era Veterans' Memorial honors the state's 1,942 known Vietnam

casualties and the 83 soldiers missing in action. Each of these soldiers' names is inscribed in the monument's black marble. During its construction, veterans placed meaningful objects inside the 40-foot columns, including items such as purple heart and bronze star medals, a P-38 can opener, and a chunk of granite representing the toughness of a unit that suffered heavy casualties. The 28-by-15 foot flag was carried by veterans on an 83-day journey—one day for each soldier missing in action—around Florida before being hoisted between the two columns.

ALFRED B. MACLAY STATE GARDENS

About 100 varieties of camellias and over 50 varieties of azaleas are the show stoppers in this state park, but there are also more than 160 other species of exotic and native plants on display. Situated on a hillside overlooking pristine Lake Hall, the property was once home to New York financier Alfred B. Maclay. Mrs. Maclay donated the property to the state in 1953.

Alligators—and lots of them. That's what visitors remember about Wakulla Springs. In all, about 400 of these bathing beauties, ranging in size from 3 inches to 14 feet, live within the boundaries of the 2,860-acre state park. Photo courtesy of the Florida Department of Commerce, Division of Tourism.

The ornamental gardens capitalize on each season's blooming beauties creating a flowering extravaganza throughout the year. In addition to the plants, native animals such as birds, deer, bobcat, fox, alligators, turtles, and fish make the gardens their home.

WAKULLA SPRINGS LODGE AND CONFERENCE CENTER

Indians relied on the Wakulla Spring for medicinal purposes; when Ponce de Leon and Spanish explorers stumbled upon it, they first thought it was the coveted fountain of youth. Yet neither of these early inhabitants realized the true mysteries buried within its depths. Dating back to 35 million years ago, the area's limestone foundation is a maze of underground rivers and caves, and geologists are still unable to pinpoint the origin of the spring. Almost directly under the lodge, divers have discovered a grand cavern tall enough to enclose a 16-story building, while scattered throughout the bottom of the spring are exotic living crustaceans and fossilized bones of prehistoric mastodons.

Today, alligators, birds, deer, turtles, snakes, and alligator gar are just a sprinkling of the wildlife inside the park.

The late financier Edward Ball bought the undeveloped land in 1933, and two years later began construction on a 27-room lodge open to the public. Glass-bottom and jungle cruise boat tours went into commission, a restaurant serving regional cuisine was opened, and because the spring water is a constant 70 degrees year round, a swimming area featuring a three-tiered diving platform was created. The lodge soon became the stomping grounds for up-and-coming politicians, business tycoons, and even military leaders such as United States General George Patton and French Colonel Charles de Gaulle.

Although the state purchased the pristine wilderness area in 1986, the park almost mirrors its image of 50 years ago. A dip at the marble soda fountain or a walk along the park's nature trails remain popular as afternoon excursions. And under the blanket of a night unbroken by neon signs and flashing billboards, the lonesome wail of the loon echoing across the spring still lulls lodge guests to sleep.

FSU "FLYING HIGH" CIRCUS

Florida State may be the only university in the nation to give credits for clowning around. Composed of students turned amateur circus performers, this big-top circus offers a stage and aerial presentation rivaling any professional circus, without the use of animals. Tight-rope walkers, jugglers, clowns, and gymnasts are among the performers in the show's 18 to 22 acts—all performed under a big-top circus tent.

The circus was started in 1947 by Jack Haskin, who was looking for a coed activity for the women on campus and the men who were just returning from the war. Today, the circus performs at FSU as well as throughout the Southeast.

UNION BANK

Built in 1841, the Union Bank is one of the few buildings to survive a fire that destroyed downtown Tallahassee in 1843. Before its restoration in 1984, it served as a freedman's bank for emancipated slaves, a church, a shoe factory, a dance studio, a beauty shop, and a bakery.

This charming structure appears to be created from blue stone, but it is actually a brick building stuccoed on the outside and then scored to look like big blocks of masonry.

SAINT MARKS NATIONAL WILDLIFE REFUGE

The 65,000 acres preserved in the Saint Marks National Wildlife Refuge show Florida at its best. Throughout the year, about 300 bird species, 50 types of reptiles and amphibians, and over 40 kinds of mammals live in the refuge. In the winter, the wetlands, palm hammocks, and scrubby forests become nesting grounds for migrating birds, including breath-taking Canadian geese.

Lighthouse Road, the main access into the refuge, leads to its namesake, a registered historic site that overlooks the Saint Marks River. Visible from the top of the Capitol on a clear day, the lighthouse has guided mariners in Apalachee Bay and the Gulf since 1831.

PEBBLE HILL PLANTATION

Just off Highway 319 between Tallahassee and Thomasville sits a large brick house only a few feet from the road. The sign posted in the yard reads "Pebble Hill Plantation," but from the looks of the building, it's hard to believe that this was ever a grand plantation at all—that is, until you realize that the brick structure is only the gate house to the more than 3,000 acres that make up the complex.

For many years, Pebble Hill was the winter home of the Hannas from Cleveland. Elisabeth Ireland Poe, better known as "Miss Pansy," was the last of the Hanna heirs and an avid sportswoman. Throughout the house, carvings and sculptures of her dogs and horses command as much attention as the prime antiques, crystal, and porcelain.

HAVANA

This charming old town, once a prosperous agricultural center specializing in tobacco leaf for cigars, is now synonymous with antiquing. Only 10 minutes north of Tallahassee, many of the restored buildings lining the narrow main street, as well as some of the town's older homes, display interesting and impressive collections of antiques. Other unusual shops specializing in dolls, ethnic items, and rocks and crystals can also be found throughout town.

BRADLEY'S COUNTRY STORE

Step back in time with a visit to Bradley's Country Store, which has been a Tallahassee landmark since 1927. Although dry goods and commodities are available for purchase, the store's claim to fame is the tasty, seasoned sausage made from Grandma Mary's 1910 recipe. Legend has it that at one time, Mary's husband would sell her sausage on the Capitol steps.

Recognized as a historic site by the National Register of Historic Places in 1984, the store is housed in its original 1927 tin roof building. ◆

—Heidi Tyline King

Lighthouse Road, the main access into the Saint Marks National Wildlife Refuge, leads to a registered historic site that overlooks the Saint Marks River. Visible from the top of the Capitol on a clear day, the lighthouse has guided mariners in Apalachee Bay and the Gulf since 1831. Photo by Robert M. Overton.

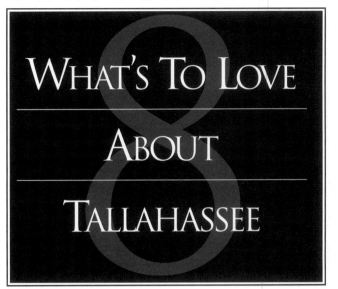

WHAT'S TO LOVE
ABOUT
TALLAHASSEE

HIDDEN TREASURES:
SOUTHERN ACCENTS AND
OLD COUNTRY ROADS

◆

*Throughout a century and a half
of growth, Tallahassee has
maintained its Southern charm,
its hospitality, and has kept its feel
of "small-town South," a quality
and character that its inhabitants
defend staunchly even today . . . ."*

—From *Yesterday's Tallahassee,*
by Hampton Dunn

◆

*Tallahassee has an undying respect for green space and the great
outdoors. Canopied roads literally create a curtain of green over
the city. Photo by Robert M. Overton.*

"The hallmark of Tallahassee is the nurturing atmosphere it provides families to flourish and create cherished memories so indicative of its style." Photo by Robert M. Overton.

And then there are the ever-present towering pines that dot the landscape north, south, east, and west. Most people have never seen such a gathering within the Florida state line. There's the moment of being awestruck on Roberts Road as drivers on a clear day notice the wide expanses of green pastures dominated by giant oak trees, each limb draped in gray, shawl-like moss.

And any day—cold or warm—could spark a bit of curiosity in those seeing the old gent whose rustic barn sits alongside Meridian Road, a handmade sign advertising his "Fix-it Shop" with its display of lawn mowers and hubcaps. There he stands, leaning against a barn door, watching the world—and you—go by.

Tallahassee is a city of contrasts, where you're likely to find uptown symphony orchestras just as popular as cracker-box "jook" joints with their window displays of neon beer signs on Bannerman Road.

And the same people who might be found jamming at the American Legion with Tom and the Cats on one night, on another night might be taking a quiet stroll up town, stopping in at Andrew's Upstairs to hear some jazz tunes or heading out to Dave's CC Club for a healthy dose of rhythm and blues.

Some might say Tallahassee has its peculiarities. But all added up, they blend together to charm visitors and residents alike.

IN THE SOUTHERN TRADITION

There's a joke that says the farther north you go from Miami, the farther south you get. It's true. The accents found in north Florida are tinged with a bit of south Georgia. It's where you'll find a woman behind the wheel of a big four-wheel drive vehicle sporting a sticker on the back bumper: "Real women drive trucks." And yet, there are times when a person would swear Tallahassee had more BMWs and Lexuses per capita than any other city in the Sunshine State.

To better know Tallahassee, one could follow the various roads leading like spokes of a wheel from the center city. Follow one through town and see the chain of parks which received a face-lift in 1994, a monument to mark Tallahassee's undying respect for green spaces and the great outdoors. The renovation includes brick-paved sidewalks, inviting benches, and a multitude of shady spots including a gazebo. There's a return to angled parking and the addition of "bump outs," helping downtown to regain a sense of pedestrian friendliness.

To the immediate south there are neighborhoods like the FAMU Addition, with homes that have been handed down through the families as many as five times over. There are the newer neighborhoods to the northeast—large expanses of land that have been carved up into developments—each with its own personality: traditional, upscale, modest, or mix. And manufactured housing

There are four seasons to a year, but to Tallahasseeans there are a great deal more. Within each season, numerous sights, sounds, tastes, and events help mark the calendar year. There's the season of plantation-style picnics at the homes of Tallahassee notables. There's the season to take weekend dips in one of the sinks among the trails located south of town.

And the season when a young bank vice president becomes a weekend widow as her husband and his pals prefer Labradors, shiny shotguns, and Eddie Bauer camouflage to yard work and other family obligations.

Of course, in Tallahassee there's also a time of budding Bradford pear trees, or the same trees' burst of bright orange and yellow before they drop their leaves—sometimes delayed until the winter months. There's one of the favorite seasons when azaleas spill over with color, and dogwoods burst forth in pink and white blooms.

In addition to season-related events, there are also perennial images of Tallahassee that give it a sense of time and place all its own. The early Saturday morning gatherings of runners and bikers during Gulf Winds Track Club's foot races and triathlons, the athletes' attire—warm or sparse—matching the temperatures.

communities, scattered on the outskirts of town, provide an entirely different living experience.

A hint of Tallahassee is found in a variety of images: its surroundings, social occasions, and backdrop.

Here, a person might discover a little-known neighborhood behind the southside police substation where it seems time has stood still. There's a very rural feel, with a general store at the center—no sign marking its existence—old cracker-box size houses with cars propped up by bricks in the driveway. Dirt trails are evidence of well-traveled pathways among neighbors and friends.

A very different discovery, also well-hidden, are Golden Eagle-style golf course homes and the lakefront bungalows and estates on Talquin, Jackson, Iamonia, or Bradford.

TALENTED TYPES

Tallahassee boasts a highly educated populace—something that is revealed through the readings by local poets and authors at a standing-room-only cafe and in the Sunday afternoon barrage of parents, children, college students, senior citizens, and more at the main branch of the Leon County Library.

It's talented, too. There's the multimedium artistic talent of Sandy Proctor with his stone sculptures, water colors, and oils. And musically, there's the wildly talented singer Pam Laws, pianist Marvin Goldstein, and a bit more folksy with original performances— John Paul Walters.

There are also the unforgettably poignant portraits by Ray Stanyard, a Tallahassee-based professional photographer, and numerous local artists-in-waiting whose work wins display at LeMoyne Art Gallery.

Tallahassee's literary talent comes in many forms: amateur—as what shows up frequently on the *Tallahassee Democrat's* opinion page—and professional, including the works of novelist Janet Burroway and fiction specialist Jerry Stern.

TIME OUT AND TIMING

A little bit of Tallahassee can be seen in the small groups of young teenagers, gathered on a Saturday afternoon at the greenery-accented Hopkins' Eatery. Or the well-dressed 40-somethings taking in dinner at the far-out (as far as distance is concerned) Nino's Italian Eatery.

As those who leave Tallahassee for career or marriage and return later in life often find, the area comes with its own special timing, as if the metronome has a notched setting for Tallahassee alone. It gives time for sharing a beer over the back fence with a neighbor, or grabbing a "time out" cup of coffee with a friend at the mall.

There are the annual parties that mark the year—which people come to expect: The Colonel's Club and the Ryals Lee New Year's Eve eve party where a person would find himself among a veritable Who's Who of the Tallahassee social register.

Such gatherings come with their own brand of social customs. Newcomers are sometimes surprised by the presumptuous manner in which they're introduced: "He's one of the Gavalas boys, you know the Nic Gavalas family, Nic's Toggery."

As transient as it might seem because of the comings and goings of college students and state government types, there's still an undercurrent of stability: old Tallahassee.

Family ties are strong in this part of the South. There are small pockets of families running several generations deep. There are the Phipps, the Hannons, the Eppes, the Hopkins, the

Tallahassee's unique characteristics blend together to charm visitors and residents alike. Photo by Robert M. Overton

Hadleys, and the Bannermans. Tallahassee Police Chief Tom Coe is a fifth generation Tallahasseean, too. And County Commissioner Manny Joanos has roots that go back to the early 1920s.

They've all stayed for love of the area. Perhaps that's why Tallahassee is often described by newcomers as "a great place to raise a family." There are more parks, green spaces, and lively playgrounds than many other towns its size. It's the kind of place where a young girl can grow up declaring her first true love was a horse and where mommies or daddies might make parenting their stay-at-home job.

WORDS BRING PERSONAL HISTORIES ALIVE

Through the years, those who have discovered Tallahassee have pursued the recording of its pleasures in both pictorial and historical representations, ranging from cookbooks and diary accounts to gift books and college dissertations.

People of Tallahassee have been writing about it for years, from the yellowed pages of the delicate book *A Century of Tallahassee Girls (1824-1924),* to the rugged tales of Robert C. Balfour Jr. in *This Land I Have Loved.*

The main branch of the Leon County Library has a quiet room closed off from the reference section that houses a collection of books, reports, and other materials detailing facts and impressions about this favored land.

It proves a love for various aspects: architecture, people, nature, history, culture, and images.

In *Yesterday's Tallahassee,* author Hampton Dunn lovingly illustrates the city's history, from the capital in the wilderness to Tallahassee since 1940. In his foreword, he says he thinks of it as his other home town. For 25 years he visited first as a political writer and later as a political commentator. "Tallahassee grows on you," he writes, "and you find yourself wanting to spend more time there."

In her chapter "Two hundred miles from anywhere else," in the book *The Other Florida,* author Gloria Jahoda says: "Tallahassee, in Leon County, is Middle Florida's metropolis and all of Florida's capital. And yet it has no orange groves, no cocktail bars, very few bikinis, no porpoises, and a history innocent of refurbishing. It lacks everything symbolic of Florida the carnival except its legislature."

In 1976 author Eleanor Ketchum wrote her dedication of *Tales of Tallahassee.* "To all who love Tallahassee, the place where spring-time begins, the dowager city of the Great State of Florida, Capital of the Sunshine State, garden spot of the whole 'Cotton pickin' world, and the Southland at its very best!" She describes Tallahassee through vignettes to give a brief glimpse of the city's historical significance, Southern charm, and gracious hospitality.

TASTES OF TALLAHASSEE

A unique book on the shelves of many long-time Tallahasseans is *The Colonel's Inn Caterers' Tallahassee Historical Cookbook,*

organized by Delia Appleyard Mickler and Carolyde Phillips O'Bryan. "This is a book about the families who came and settled in Tallahassee over a one-hundred-year period from 1824 to 1924. Many members of these families married each other, and through the years formed long and lasting kinships. It is about these people, and the homes they built and lived in, that this book is written."

The book's foreword says: "Those of us who live here feel that Tallahassee is the most beautiful city in the world. Early in the year nature opens up into springtime with its brilliant azaleas, camellias, pink buds, dogwoods, flowering quince, tulips, and daffodils in all their blaze of glory."

An index of people and places is included in the book—Call, Perkins, Strauss, as well as Bellevue, Elks Club, and The Grove—which is followed by an index of recipes. It's a true genealogy of Tallahassee's first families and their favorite eats.

Something that also captures the unique spirit of Tallahassee is the *Canopy Roads* cookbook, a treasure collected by the Junior Woman's Club, where men have a section of recipes all their own. One entry, for example, is Buttermilk Fried Mullet, "very delicious at breakfast or anytime served with grits," says contributor Bill Rowan. "It has a taste all its own."

And in the proper Southern tradition, some women will still be referred to according to their husband's name, as in the reference "Mrs. Charles Miner (Judy)."

There's a special section for dignitaries, where cooks will find recipes from the likes of Donna Lou Askew, wife of former Governor Reubin Askew (1970-1978), and Adele Graham, wife of former Governor Bob Graham (1978-1982), now a United States senator, as well as many Florida senators and representatives and their wives.

A bit more formal is the *Thymes Remembered* cookbook, which was organized by the Junior League of Tallahassee. A prelude says: "Every locale has its notable distinctions. Since plantation days, the charm of Tallahassee's rolling hills, beautiful flowers, and plentiful trees has beckoned many to make this city their home. The hallmark of Tallahassee is the nurturing atmosphere it provides families to flourish and create cherished memories so indicative of its style. Tallahasseeans consider their city a perfect place to call home."

Appropriately, the words are illustrated with a genteel setting of wicker chairs, a wide-brimmed, flowered hat with ribbons, pink lemonade, lace, and a scrumptious looking kiwi-raspberry-mix dessert.

This is Tallahassee, true to form. ◆

—Julie S. Bettinger

Tallahassee is noted for its plantation-style Southern charm and gracious hospitality. It is often described as "what's left of the old Florida." Photo by Robert M. Overton.

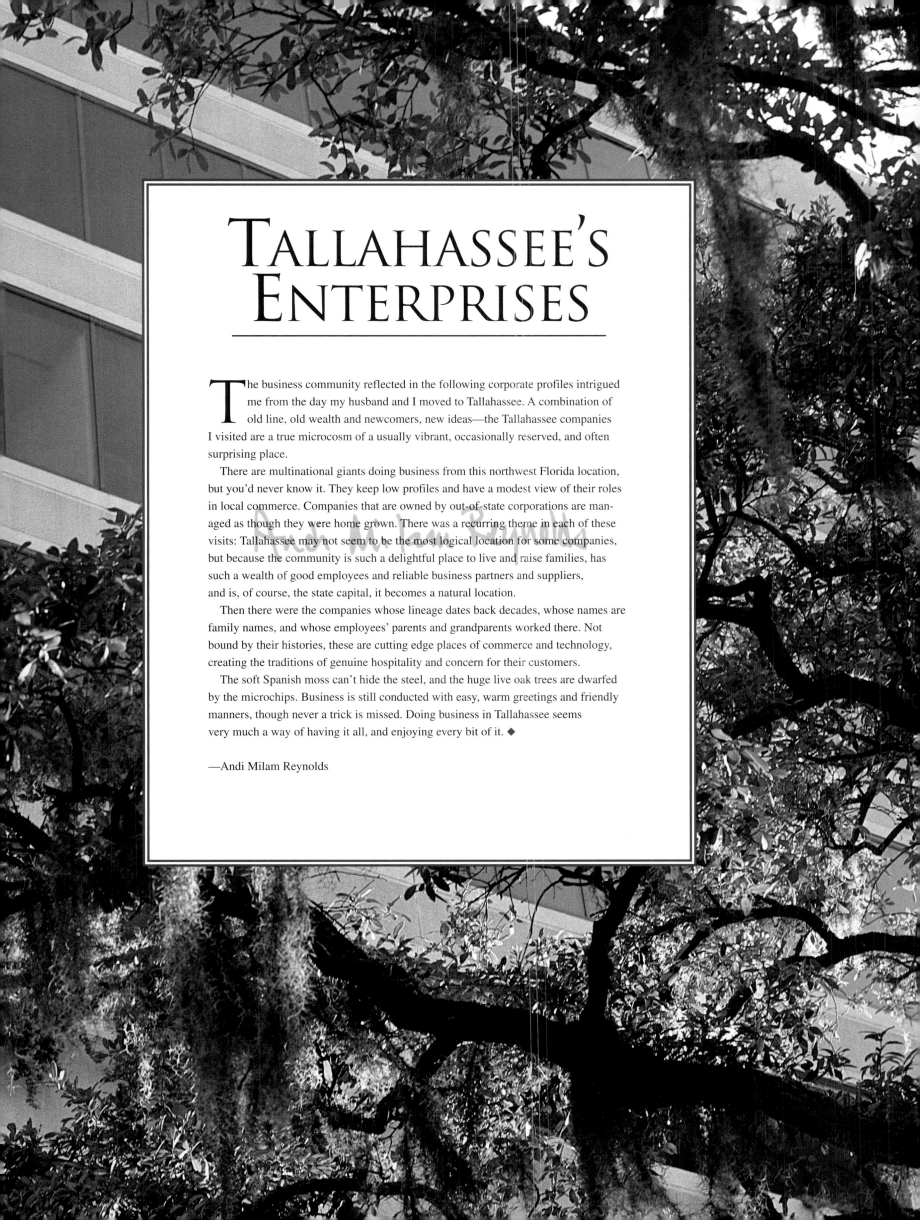

Tallahassee's Enterprises

The business community reflected in the following corporate profiles intrigued me from the day my husband and I moved to Tallahassee. A combination of old line, old wealth and newcomers, new ideas—the Tallahassee companies I visited are a true microcosm of a usually vibrant, occasionally reserved, and often surprising place.

There are multinational giants doing business from this northwest Florida location, but you'd never know it. They keep low profiles and have a modest view of their roles in local commerce. Companies that are owned by out-of-state corporations are managed as though they were home grown. There was a recurring theme in each of these visits: Tallahassee may not seem to be the most logical location for some companies, but because the community is such a delightful place to live and raise families, has such a wealth of good employees and reliable business partners and suppliers, and is, of course, the state capital, it becomes a natural location.

Then there were the companies whose lineage dates back decades, whose names are family names, and whose employees' parents and grandparents worked there. Not bound by their histories, these are cutting edge places of commerce and technology, creating the traditions of genuine hospitality and concern for their customers.

The soft Spanish moss can't hide the steel, and the huge live oak trees are dwarfed by the microchips. Business is still conducted with easy, warm greetings and friendly manners, though never a trick is missed. Doing business in Tallahassee seems very much a way of having it all, and enjoying every bit of it. ◆

—Andi Milam Reynolds

NETWORKS

◆

The area's transportation, communications, and energy firms keep people, information, and power circulating inside and outside of Tallahassee. Photo by Robert M. Overton.

Modern telecommunications came to Florida's capital city in 1895 when business-man George Schewing teamed up with George Saxon, founder of Capital City National Bank, to begin the city's first local telephone company. Total start-up investment for the enterprise was $3,400.

The fledgling firm soon attracted the attention of a prominent Tallahassee physician, Dr. W. L. Moor, who saw the new technology as a marvelous way to keep in touch with his patients. Dr. Moor and his partner, W. C. Lewis of Lewis State Bank fame, purchased the company from Schewing and Saxon and named it Southern Telephone and Construction Company.

At the end of its first year in business, the company boasted 60 subscribers, connected to each other by operators working a manual switchboard located on Monroe Street between

SPRINT/CENTEL
FLORIDA

College and Park Avenues. After several moves to various downtown buildings, the telephone company settled in 1938 to its present home at the corner of Calhoun Street and Park Avenue. That building now houses the city's main telephone switching center, handling over 130,000 customer lines, business offices, a repair center, and directory assistance operators.

By 1905 the telephone directory contained 270 listings. State government had 11 of those listings, including one for the Capitol's janitor. Also in that year, the first long distance line serving the city was completed to Monticello, where it connected to the Southern Bell circuit out of Thomasville. That single line had to meet the long distance needs of the entire area, and bottlenecks were common.

Another service the phone company provided, unique to the time, involved the city's fire alarm system. Tallahassee was divided into five districts, and phone customers were instructed to call the operator in the event of a fire and give their location and district number. The operator would then ring the alarm for the reported location, dispatching fire fighters to the scene.

Monthly residential telephone rates at the time were $2.00 for single party and $1.25 for four-party service. An additional 25 cents was charged for each half mile outside the city limits.

Tallahassee grew steadily, and by 1924 Southern Telephone and Construction was serving 1,200 area customers. It had the distinction of being the only independent, or non-Bell, telephone company in the nation serving a capital city.

As World War II dawned, the company had changed its name to "Southeastern Telephone" and was serving almost 8,000 customers. The next name change took place in the mid-70s, when Southeastern Telephone became "Central Telephone Company of Florida," part of Chicago-based Centel Corporation. When Centel merged with Sprint in 1993, the local company assumed its present title, "Sprint/Centel-Florida."

Because of Tallahassee's rapid growth and the evermore sophisticated telecommunications demands of state government and two major universities, the local telephone system has traditionally been "ahead of the curve" when it comes to technological advancements. Dial service replaced operator-connected local calling in 1950, and just a few decades later, Tallahassee became one of the first cities in the country to benefit from fully digital telephone switching. This ushered in the modern era of Touch-Tone dialing, custom calling features such as call waiting and caller ID and Messageline service, as well as an open door to the exciting future of telecommunications.

The hub of Tallahassee's telephone network has been at the corner of Park Avenue and Calhoun Street since 1938. Today's modern five-story structure actually contains the original building.

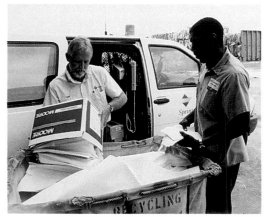

Whether recycling phone books or office paper, Sprint/Centel-Florida has aggressively pursued resource conservation. That campaign has been recognized as one of the best in Florida by numerous environmental organizations.

Although digital switching and fiber-optic transmission has made today's telecommunications more reliable than ever, problems can occur, and Sprint/Centel-Florida's Repair Center stands ready to speed service restoration.

But there was no easy or economical way to connect these networks to each other until Sprint/Centel-Florida built one of the nation's largest fiber-optic data networks. This network rings the downtown area with spokes to major remote office complexes and links more than 70 state government computer networks. This advanced technology also serves a growing number of private sector customers in business and industry.

Although part of a worldwide corporation, Sprint/Centel-Florida does its best to be a good hometown neighbor. The company is active in the Partners for Excellence program in support of local schools. The United Way of the Big Bend, the March of Dimes, the Public Broadcasting Center, and many other area organizations benefit from the company's involvement, and employee groups such as the Community Relations Team and Independent Telephone Pioneers Association devote enormous amounts of time and talent to dozens of worthy causes.

From rather humble origins at the turn of the last century, Sprint/Centel-Florida is poised to bring its capital city customers into the next century with advanced telecommunications solutions, building on a century-old tradition of service, caring, and commitment. ◆

The company supplies state government and Florida State University with sophisticated Centrex systems, eliminating the need for these customers to buy and maintain their own telephone equipment. Highly reliable and incredibly versatile, these systems routinely carry hundreds of thousands of calls per day.

At the same time, Sprint/Centel-Florida has been aggressively deploying the latest in fiber-optic technology to meet an exploding demand for both voice and data communications.

Tallahassee is the computer capital of Florida, with just over half of the state's computer power situated within a few miles of the Capitol building. State government alone operates 18 mainframe data centers, more than 250 minicomputers, 30,000 personal computers, and 23,000 terminals. Most of these are hooked up to one of more than 450 local area networks, which allows them to share information with their departmental neighbors.

Tallahassee telephone customers could choose from either wall or desk model phones in 1956, each available in "five attractive colors." That contrasts with today's incredible selection of phones and features to meet every conceivable need.

MCKENZIE TANK LINES

McKenzie Tank Lines is one of the largest bulk carriers in the nation and serves a broad spectrum of chemical, pulp and paper, and petroleum industry customers. McKenzie also transports gasoline to service stations and propane gas for industrial, commercial, and home use. The company's reputation for reliability, safety, and service is among the trucking industry's best. Their yellow tractors with the McKenzie block "M" logo are familiar to shippers throughout the continental United States, Canada, and Mexico. Safety is the reason for the tractor color, yellow having the highest nighttime visibility.

McKenzie drivers operate 500 plus tractors and over 1,000 trailers from a system of 24 terminals in Georgia, Florida, North Carolina, Texas, Alabama, and Louisiana. In Tallahassee, McKenzie manufactures stainless steel chemical tank trailers, recaps tires, operates a tractor overhaul and maintenance facility, and trains and retrains emergency responders. Most McKenzie Tallahassee activities are support in nature with a substantial operating facility being located on the Gulf Intercoastal Waterway at nearby Saint Marks, Florida. Barges deliver chemicals, fuel oil, and gasoline for subsequent transportation by McKenzie Tank Lines trucks.

McKenzie drivers are trained specifically in the products they haul. In the event of an accident or spill by McKenzie or others, the company has 13 HAZMAT emergency response teams who drive or are airlifted to the accident or spill. McKenzie teams are authorized HAZMAT responders for the Florida Highway Patrol and other public safety agencies.

Training and safety are key elements for all of the company's 1,000 plus associates. Quarterly quality meetings are held within the company and externally with customers and major suppliers such as Mack Trucks, which provides the tractors the company uses in its hauling business. McKenzie solicits input on equipment specifications and design from its drivers and mechanics. This input has helped to make the equipment safer and easier for drivers to operate.

Both Guy McKenzie Sr. and Guy McKenzie Jr. have served as officials in state and national trucking organizations. Presently, Guy Sr., company chairman, is director of the Florida Trucking Association, and Guy Jr., McKenzie's president, serves as chairman of the National Tank Truck Carriers, the national industry trade association.

In the community, McKenzie sponsors and makes contributions to those organizations in which its employee associates and their children and grandchildren are involved, such as FSU, FAMU, local high schools, athletic teams, and academic competitions. McKenzie offers a student loan program open to any employee associate's child or grandchild for higher educational or vocational studies. ◆

The company's reputation for reliability, safety, and service is among the trucking industry's best.

The yellow tractors with the McKenzie block "M" logo are familiar to shippers throughout the continental United States, Canada, and Mexico.

Comcast Cable has come a long way in the 30 years since the company began offering cable television service in Tupelo, Mississippi. Now, the Philadelphia-based company is the third largest television operator in the United States, offering service in 18 states and over 500 communities, reaching more than 3 million subscribers.

But Comcast is more than a television company. Through its diversification program, the company has evolved into a leadership position in the area of high-technology communications. In addition to cable, Comcast is one of the nation's leading wireless cellular telephone providers. The

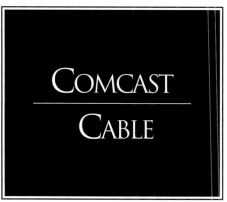

COMCAST CABLE

company serves a heavily traveled corridor with a population of 7.4 million, stretching from northern New Jersey to southern Delaware, with Philadelphia as its anchor. In addition to wireless telephones, Comcast also provides residential telephone service overseas, particularly in the United Kingdom. At home, Comcast's cable infrastructure is the foundation of its involvement in another exciting field. Cable has the potential to transmit data 1,000 times faster than existing telephone lines, providing greater capacity and efficiency. This means that computer users could soon have uninterrupted access to the Internet and other information services. In recognition of the value content providers offer in today's multichannel world, the company has programming investments in E: Entertainment, Music Choice, Turner Broadcasting, and Viewer's Choice and is a principal shareholder in QVC.

New developments include Comcast's 30 percent share of Nextel. This communications company has a potential service area of 180 million people and will transmit voice, data, and alphanumeric messaging using digital technology. Other technology partners include Motorola, Northern Telecom, and Nippon Telephone and Telegraph.

Comcast's goal is to provide its customers with the power to communicate from anywhere to anywhere else on the planet, whether by satellite, television cable, fiber optics, digital electronics, cellular radio, or by techniques still on the drawing board. The company intends to meet each subscriber's every communications need in entertainment, information, and telephone at home, at work, and while traveling.

Even as the company continues to blaze new trails in competitive telecommunications services, management remains committed to the belief that Comcast's principle strength is involvement in each community served. Tallahassee is no exception. A multimillion dollar system rebuild is under way to bring twenty-first-century communication services to Florida's capital city today.

The company is a major employer in the high-tech sector of the area's economy and a strong corporate citizen, sponsoring such events as the Big Bend Saltwater Classic and supporting organizations as diverse as the Organization for Artificial Reefs, the Leon County Public Library, the Dick Howser Center, and the Tallahassee Museum of History and Natural Science. In addition, Comcast wired all of the schools in its service area for Cable in the Classroom, an effort by the cable industry to provide commercial-free, educational programming with no copyright restrictions.

Comcast feels its presence in Tallahassee is important, because the city is the state capital, the area is one of Florida's major markets, and there is a burgeoning hotbed of technological development on the horizon via the universities. With Comcast's provision of superior cable and communications services, Tallahassee is assured of having the latest and finest infrastructure and services to meet any business or individual needs. ◆

From its first broadcast in 1955, WCTV Channel 6 has been the leader in local and regional television news and entertainment programming in the North Florida/South Georgia area. A commitment to using the latest in technology and innovative programming has made WCTV the highest ranked regional source for news, weather, sports, and entertainment among all locally available media.

A CBS affiliate, WCTV was founded by the late John H. Phipps. The station is owned by the Phipps family and is managed and operated by John H. Phipps, Inc. Just as the station's history is one of family ownership, so is its tradition one of deep community involvement and public service. On-air personalities are well-known and highly respected residents from Tallahassee and surrounding towns, including Thomasville, Georgia, the station's original site.

The intimate connection between residents and the station is evident in the popularity of WCTV's local programming. The "Good Morning Show," an hour of local, regional, state, and national news and local features, is an important beginning to the day for thousands of area viewers. At noon, WCTV provides the area's only middle-of-the-day television news with "Mid-Day." In the evening, WCTV provides viewers with three news broadcasts—"Eyewitness News" at 5:30 P.M., 6:00 P.M., and 11:00 P.M. WCTV recently made part of its 24-hour broadcasting more accessible to the area's citizens who are hearing impaired by making all three of its evening broadcasts closed-cationed.

WCTV takes pride in helping the people and communities it serves by promoting and highlighting the events and activities important to them. One of the most notable

From its first broadcast in 1955, WCTV Channel 6 has been the leader in local and regional television news and entertainment programming in the North Florida/South Georgia area.

examples of the impact the station has had on the lives of its audience is its unique monthly adopt-a-child feature. Children waiting for adoption in South Georgia and North Florida are referred to the station by those states' human service agencies. Between 60 and 70 percent of the children who have been featured discussing their hopes, dreams, and wishes for belonging to a family have been adopted. The station's interest in the community is also demonstrated in its support for such efforts as the Muscular Dystrophy Telethon, the Children's Miracle Network, and numerous other groups and organizations.

WCTV operates a state-of-the-art broadcasting facility with its 2,000-foot tower, built in 1987, providing a broadcast range of 85 miles. WCTV has the latest in severe weather forecasting and reporting ability with its on-site Doppler Color Radar System, the only system of its kind in the region. News is broadcast live from any scene via the station's Electronic News Gathering (ENG) truck. This kind of advanced technology, together with news bureaus in Tallahassee,

A commitment to using the latest in technology and innovative programming has made WCTV the highest ranked regional source for news, weather, sports, and entertainment among all locally available media sources.

Thomasville, and Valdosta, Georgia, allows WCTV to give viewers the best television news coverage in the area.

Using innovative programming, talented and skilled on-air and behind-the-scenes staff, and the latest in technology, WCTV has won numerous Associated Press News Awards recognizing excellence in broadcast news journalism and Addy Awards for outstanding achievement in local commercial advertising and production.

The history of WCTV Channel 6, 40 years old in 1995, and the outlook for its future are best summed up by the corporate logo, the charter oak, which represents stability, longevity, strength, and growth, and WCTV's motto, "In Service To The Community." ◆

BUSINESS & FINANCE

◆

Business is still conducted with friendly manners in Tallahassee.
Photo by Robert M. Overton.

The Tallahassee Area Chamber of Commerce is the voice of Tallahassee's business community. With 1,400 members and more signing on each year, the Chamber enjoys a higher-than-average membership ratio for communities the size of Tallahassee and Leon County. That's because for over 70 years, the Chamber has been in step with the times.

TALLAHASSEE AREA CHAMBER OF COMMERCE

The Chamber's two primary responsibilities are economic development and service to existing businesses. In pursuit of the first, the Chamber and the City of Tallahassee in 1991 entered into formation of Project 2010, a joint private/public-funded program to attract new high-value jobs to the Tallahassee area. In its first three years, Project 2010 not only drew new enterprises to the community, but was also instrumental in enabling several existing firms to remain here rather than transfer their operations elsewhere.

Examination of the Chamber's list of chairmen from the early 1920s until today shows it has been directed by the leading figures of Florida's capital city. A veritable who's who of prominent personalities have, as Chamber chairs, guided this progressive community through good times and bad, wars and economic depressions, social upheaval and political strife. Through it all, the Chamber was a stabilizing force of leadership.

That tradition has prevailed in recent years. The Chamber led the campaign to build Tallahassee's Civic Center, the Florida State University Center for Professional Development (now the Turnbull Center), and the Adams Street Commons. Tallahassee's principal high technology private industries—General Dynamics and its affiliate Talla-Com—came to Tallahassee through a Chamber initiative. And the Chamber strives to attract industries that can capitalize on the town's most dramatic scientific asset, the National High Magnetic Field Laboratory, unequaled anywhere in the world.

The personnel of the Tallahassee Area Chamber of Commerce help carry forth the Chamber's rich tradition of business representation and community improvement. The staff includes: (left to right, first row) Tina Campbell, Amy Herring, Linda Powell, Kelly Hartung, Brenda Herring, (second row) Brenda Davis, Camille Bielby, Gina Rhodes, Callie Melton, (third row) Jim Ashlock, Dick Kuehl, and Joe Kelley.

In its role as business advocate, the Chamber has appeared frequently before city and county commissions, fighting for businesses that needed help in overcoming regulatory snags or short-sighted public opposition to development plans.

But the Chamber's activities extend well beyond these two important assignments. It is in the forefront of female empowerment, sponsoring the highly popular Women's Forum each month where prominent speakers address topics of interest to business and professional women. Indeed, the time is near when the Chamber will have the first woman chairing its board of directors.

Business After Hours, sponsored each month by a leading business establishment, is the Chamber's most popular "mixer." Hundreds of local business figures regularly attend BAH to network and otherwise provide cohesiveness to the local business scene.

As with most such organizations, small businesses constitute the largest percentage of Tallahassee Chamber membership. That's why the Chamber annually sponsors the Small Business Awards Banquet, where honors are bestowed on the year's top entrepreneurial achievers.

Highlights of the annual social season are the Chamber's "Welcome Back" reception opening each session of the Florida legislature and the black tie balls honoring the Speaker of the House of Representatives and President of the Senate.

Housed within the Chamber's headquarters in a beautiful antebellum mansion, known locally as the Columns, are other vital community services. Keep Tallahassee/Leon County Beautiful is dedicated to the area's environmental welfare. Partners for Excellence and the Schools Foundation are the Chamber's links with the Leon County Board of Education, promoting teacher/student recognition and school quality. Another tenant is the Downtown Improvement Authority, fostering city-center investments.

This rich tradition of business representation and community improvement will guide the Tallahassee Chamber as it leads the march toward greater achievements in the twenty-first century. ◆

PAST CHAIRMEN

Tallahassee Area Chamber of Commerce

T. J. Appleyard	1923-1925
Irvin Gates	1926
Frank D. Moor	1927-1928
Lewis M. Lively	1929
Payne H. Midyette	1930
Jack W. Simmons	1931
G. E. Lewis	1932
J. A. Cawthon	1933
L. D. Fain	1934
Frank S. Shaw	1935
Fred N. Lowry	1936
Ralph E. Proctor	1937
Charles S. Ausley	1938
Rainy Cawthon	1939
F. Wilson Carraway	1940
Godfrey Smith*	1941
Benson Skelton	1941
Phelps W. Long	1942
John M. Tapers	1943
Moseley C. Collins	1944
J. Velma Keen	1945-1946
Al B. Block	1947
J. Velma Keen	1948
J. Kenneth Ballinger	1949
John Y. Humphress	1950
M. Julian Proctor	1951
Ed M. Clark	1952
Ben C. Willis	1953
Louis Hill	1954
Ed Steinmeyer	1955
Blair Stone	1956
Judd W. Chapman	1957
Fred O. Drake Jr.	1958
J. D. Williamson	1959
R. Spencer Burress	1960
Ernest Menendez	1961
H. Jack Yaeger Jr.	1962
Payne H. Midyette Jr.	1963
W. Paul Shelley	1964
Frank M. Dennis	1965
Gene Berkowitz	1966
Robert T. Brinkley	1967
James E. Joanos	1968
William P. Malloy	1969
C. Dubose Ausley	1970
Edward K. Walker	1971
Bernie Shiell	1972

The Chamber's headquarters are housed within the beautiful antebellum mansion, known locally as the Columns. Painting by Richard Lewis.

Bill Cartee	1973
Chever Lewis	1974
Ryals Lee	1975-1976
Elliot Messer	1977-1978
Taylor Moore	1979-1980
Roger Smith	1981
Tom Perrin	1982
Brent Pichard	1983
George Lingford	1984
William L. Sutton	1985
Robert W. West	1986
Bruce Culpepper	1987
Lawton Chiles III	1988
John R. Lewis	1989
Ivan Johnson	1990
John Perry Thomas	1991
Ronald La Face	1992
Frank Shaw Jr.	1993
J. Everitt Drew Jr.	1994

* Entered military service

FRINGE BENEFITS MANAGEMENT COMPANY

Fringe Benefits Management Company (FBMC) is a progressive and responsible Florida-based, independently owned corporation that provides third-party administrative services to public and private employers throughout the United States. It is also one of the largest private sector employers in Tallahassee.

Fringe Benefits Management Company was founded in 1976. The company's 12 years of top quality third-party flexible benefit plan administration began in 1982, when Dade County Public Schools, the fourth largest school district in the country, awarded FBMC the contract to administer the Dade County Public Schools' flexible benefit plan. Fringe Benefits Management Company continues to provide service to school boards nationwide in addition to its private sector clients and state, county, and local government clients. The company's current clients include such prestigious accounts as the States of New York, Wisconsin, North Carolina, West Virginia, Arkansas, Louisiana, and California. Fringe Benefits Management Company now provides service to a combined eligible employee population that is rapidly approaching one million.

Michael H. Sheridan, Fringe Benefit Management Company's visionary president and one of the company's founders, organized the company under a nontraditional, team-based, matrix management system. Sheridan takes pride in his firm's ability to adapt to the fluid business landscape and tells his employees that the only promise he can make to them is that change will occur. "The success of any business in the future lies in meeting the needs of the marketplace and exceeding the expectations of the customer. Changes in these needs and expectations are so rapid that getting a staid business like an insurance brokerage and benefits management company to respond quickly is quite challenging."

"Our employees are our best recruiters," says Michael Sheridan, president and founder of Fringe Benefits Management Company. In 1993 Fringe Benefits Management Company was the first Tallahassee company to receive the Governor's Business Leadership Award, one of only nine such awards given throughout Florida.

While most competitors present clients with generic products and services, FBMC's effort to master the changing market landscape centers on quality products and custom services designed to meet the unique needs of each individual client. From insurance brokerage to benefits administration to claims payment administration to retirement planning, each business activity is tailored to fit the specific needs of FBMC's client and the client's employees.

The company's industry-leading innovations include products such as the Customized Benefits Management package, the *VISTA* Benefits Management System, HealthQuest, and their state-of-the-art Benefits Communication system.

These innovations, as well as many others, were developed by FBMC's own, in-house, team of product developers and are the result of open communication with clients and their employees. They have been achieved using Total Quality Management tools. The entire company operates under the principles of Total Quality Management. This means that from the president to entry-level staff, all work is performed with user satisfaction as the paramount objective. FBMC is visibly committed to continual improvement as well as the development of new services and products to fill the needs of the changing marketplace.

The firm has set the pace in the industry with such innovations as dedicated FAX lines that feed directly into the company's reimbursement department and reduce the turn-around time for claims payment, direct deposit of claims payment, and TDD service for the hearing impaired. Other innovations include improved data accuracy from electronic payroll data transfer and a 24-hour legal bulletin board service used for posting questions and reports concerning benefit program compliance issues and legislative changes.

To FBMC, superior performance is not mere rhetoric. It's a corporate culture. The company offers its clients award-winning performance guarantees that are backed by significant financial penalties if the contractual standards are not met. Not only that; if any of the company's individual employees feel that a customer was inconvenienced or did not receive the level of service to which FBMC aspires for any reason, that employee is empowered to sign and send an "OOPS check" to the affected customer. These checks are in increments of $5.00 and, like the financial penalties associated with the performance guarantees, are drawn directly from the company's employee bonus pool. Thus, the performance of any single FBMC employee affects the bottom line for every other FBMC employee. The result of these programs has been a

Fringe Benefits Management Company is centered on project and performance teams that bring the force of the combined creativity, experience, and problem solving ability of representatives from each of the company's departments together.

tremendous sense of teamwork and a dramatic increase in the company's performance.

Fringe Benefits Management Company's nontraditional internal organization is centered on project and performance teams that bring the force of the combined creativity, experience, and problem solving ability of representatives from each of the company's departments together to analyze the effectiveness of policies, processes, and procedures; develop new products; and solve problems. Client representatives also sit as team members to provide input and assure their satisfaction with the outcomes of team projects.

Empowering employees with the authority to make decisions, along with the responsibility for the results, has been made easier because of the quality of Tallahassee's work force. With two universities and a community college fueling the labor pool, the requisite business skills, computer programming skills, and communication skills are available in a population that has the desire to influence corporate decisions. Tallahassee's overhead costs are low, allowing FBMC to offer reasonable wages in a low-margin, high-volume business.

In addition to its progressive management and operations profile, Fringe Benefits Management Company is ahead of many firms in its commitment to affirmative action and equal employment. "Our employees are our best recruiters," says Sheridan. "Our employees' enthusiasm about their jobs, performance standards, and the company speaks volumes about how right our approach has been." In both 1992 and 1993, the company's exemplary efforts in equal employment opportunity and affirmative action were recognized by the Florida Commission on Human Relations, which presented a certificate of appreciation to Sheridan and invited him to speak at the Florida Civil Rights Conference.

FBMC has repeatedly demonstrated its commitment to providing a worker-friendly environment, from flexible scheduling to the choice of a home office location served by public transportation. The firm's choice of location, in fact, demonstrates another level of commitment—the commitment to the Tallahassee community. The corporate offices are located in an area targeted for revitalization, and FBMC's status as

a visionary participant in Tallahassee's future economic development is demonstrated by the company's activity in both the Tallahassee Southside Pilot Revitalization Project and the Southside Commerce Association. The company is socially responsible and both encourages and recognizes employee participation in charitable, environmental, and community improvement activities.

These elements—a progressive management style, open external relationships, dedication to community, and the development of innovative approaches in a tradition-bound industry—have garnered FBMC considerable attention and resulted in several awards. *Inc.* magazine has profiled FBMC's rigorous performance guarantees as "guarantees with teeth," and the firm has been featured in the "Customer Service Manager's Newsletter," an industry bible. In 1993 Fringe Benefits Management Company was the first Tallahassee company to receive the Governor's Business Leadership Award, one of only nine such awards given throughout Florida.

The impact of FBMC's uniqueness in relation to the rest of the industry has been a fairly consistent 25-percent annual growth rate with the company tripling in size every five years. Among the company's employees this growth has reinforced the need for rapid response to industry changes.

Fringe Benefits Management Company has anticipated and, in fact, even precipitated past changes in the benefits industry. In these times of wide-ranging state and national benefit reforms, Sheridan's promise of change stands inevitable in its fulfillment. There is little doubt that the company will continue as an industry leader and innovator. ◆

The firm has set the pace in the industry with such innovations as a 24-hour legal bulletin board service used for posting questions and reports concerning benefit program compliance issues and legislative changes.

MHI GROUP, INC.

It is MHI Group's vision to be recognized as having earned the reputation of being the leader in the death care industry. The company embarked on this endeavor in September of 1987 with the purchase of the Star of David Memorial Gardens Cemetery and Funeral Home in Fort Lauderdale. Since then, MHI Group has seen its vision become reality, owning properties in Florida and Colorado. It has become recognized as an innovator and leader in marketing consumers' funeral arrangements prior to death (pre-need) and has also established itself as a leader in meeting the consumers' funeral needs at the time of death (at-need).

The company's funeral homes offer a complete range of services, including family consultation, the planning and arrangement of funeral services, the sale of caskets and related merchandise, the removal and preparation of remains, the use of funeral home facilities for visitation, worship, and tribute, the preparation of legal documents, transportation services, and aftercare services, such as support groups and self-help information. In addition, MHI Group offers cremation services to families and other funeral homes. Cemetery products offered include grave sites, lawn crypts, mausoleum crypts, cremation memorial niches, caskets, burial vaults, markers, memorials, and interment services.

MHI Group is recognized as an innovator and leader in marketing consumers' funeral arrangements. Shown here is Oakley Funeral Home in Dade City, Florida.

With such a wide array of decisions to make, the pre-need concept is especially attractive, allowing families the opportunity to logically plan their own funeral arrangements in a nongrieving environment, thereby easing the burden on family members later. A pre-need contract, which may be paid for in installments, can include the entire funeral and cemetery arrangement.

It is meeting this pre-need demand that has largely given MHI Group an average annual growth of over 20 percent since it entered the industry, and revenue growth of approximately 300 percent since September of 1987. Additional demand for services comes from MHI Group's combination concept, where funeral home services are linked to cemetery properties. The convenience and reduced cost for customers are very attractive.

The only company headquartered in Tallahassee that is listed on the New York Stock Exchange, MHI Group's location in the state capital gives it good positioning in the death care industry in Florida. Tallahassee provides the company with a pool of qualified employees, a very livable community, and access to state government, important in an industry that is heavily regulated to protect consumers. Florida has the nation's oldest population, which has a heavy demand for funeral services. North Florida is also centrally located to the southeast states that have laws favorable to pre-need marketing, as well as anticipated demand for services with their growing retiree populations. The company markets its services through referrals, direct mail campaigns, telemarketing, seminars, and media advertising.

Rather than build or develop new funeral homes and cemetery properties, MHI Group prefers to expand or synergize by acquiring existing properties and their management, staff, and facilities. MHI Group acquires properties in states where trust laws are conducive to marketing pre-need funeral and cemetery services and products, and where combination ownership of funeral homes, cemeteries, and crematories is permitted. The company seeks established businesses that have well-respected reputations, traditions, and heritage in their communities, and key management that is highly regarded and motivated to join with MHI Group.

These strategies have paid off, making MHI Group a very well regarded company in the death care industry. In July of 1993, *Florida Trend* ranked the company 16th on measurements of growth in income, sales, and return on equity among the state's largest public companies. The *Miami Herald* listed MHI Group 32 out of the state's top 100 publicly held companies on similar measures in May of 1993, including rankings of fourth best return on sales and tenth for average return on shareholder equity. At

Rather than build or develop new funeral homes and cemetery properties, MHI Group prefers to expand or synergize by acquiring existing properties such as Chapel Hill Gardens in Dade City, Florida.

the same time, the *Tampa Tribune* ranked MHI Group first in income from continuing operations as a percentage of revenue, second in one-year average return on equity, and third in change in income as a percentage of revenues, with an overall rank of eighth among Florida's top 50 publicly held companies. The company was one of five finalists and received an honorable mention in the 1994 Blue Chip Enterprise program for exemplary small businesses in America sponsored by Connecticut Mutual and *Nation's Business* magazine.

Much of MHI's bottom line success is attributable to the company's approach to staff development and training. The company provides extensive training for its operations staff for several reasons: succession planning, which promotes field staff to corporate positions; personal development to retain good employees and help them become better at what they do; and to meet MHI Group's unique organizational structure needs. Rather than add layers of middle management, the company expands responsibilities at the local level and strengthens support from the corporate level. Operations personnel have the autonomy and authority to carry out their responsibilities. To fulfill this empowerment concept, local staff are cross-trained in every aspect of their operations, and many properties are run by work teams rather than single individuals. Its unique management style has garnered MHI Group recognition for its human resources innovations in *The Director,* the magazine of the National Funeral Directors Association.

The tradition of the funeral industry is active involvement in communities, and MHI Group properties continue this heritage. Schools and community groups in locations where the company's funeral homes, cemeteries, and crematories are located receive the benefit of MHI Group's involvement in activities at individual and property levels. In Tallahassee, agencies and

organizations such as the American Cancer Society, March of Dimes, Tallahassee Memorial Regional Medical Center, United Way, and the Chamber of Commerce have enjoyed MHI Group support, sponsorship, or participation.

Through its favorable location, strong marketing, leadership in service, and effective management techniques, MHI Group is accomplishing its mission: to Manage the company in such a manner as to maximize shareholders' equity; to Help all families who place their trust in the company to the best of its professional capability; and to Improve the quality of life for all members of the company. ◆

The only company headquartered in Tallahassee that is listed on the New York Stock Exchange, MHI Group's location in the state capital gives it good positioning in the death care industry in Florida.

CAPITAL CITY
BANK

Born in a sluggish economic year, Capital City Bank opened its doors in 1895 and prosperity soon followed. A familiar fixture on Tallahassee's financial scene, Capital City has been noted for its ability to build customer relationships, financial strength, and quality service.

In the beginning, financing farming operations proved to be the bank's primary business. Capital City also backed ventures in cotton production and the turpentine and lumber industries. Today, Capital City's financial presence within its market areas includes retail banking, corporate banking, mortgage banking, and trust and investment services. The bank has played a vital role in Florida's capital city as it evolved from dependence on a few major industries to a more highly diversified mixture of manufacturing, service, and technology.

Much of the bank's success can be attributed to its founder,

Capital City Bank was one of the first banks in the nation to provide its customers with a mobile ATM which travels to local community events and functions.

George W. Saxon. The principles that have guided the company through 100 years of depressions, recessions, booms and busts, natural disasters, and two world wars began with this early entrepreneur. Those principles have been carried on by Godfrey Smith, whose career with Capital City began in 1937.

Capital City Bank has been a steady, conservative banking leader and perennially receives Veribanc's Blue Ribbon and Green Three Star ratings for safety and soundness. The bank has also been profiled as one of the top four banks in Florida and one of the top 175 safest banks in the nation by *Money Magazine*.

This excellent performance is based on a single, simple philosophy—community banking. Deposits are collected and invested locally to individuals and businesses alike. Local decision-making authority allows Capital City's loan officers to approve loans and provide the utmost in personalized service to the bank's customers.

While the bank remains locally owned and dedicated to the community, Tallahassee has provided the bank with a good, stable base of operation. William G. Smith Jr., chairman of the board, credits much of Capital City's success to the community to which it belongs. "We've been fortunate. We live in a good town and are in good markets. Those markets have helped us grow, and we've helped them grow. Having good

Throughout the year, Capital City Bank sponsors events such as Celebrate America on the Fourth of July.

communities for our associates to work and live in is equally important to us while we endeavor to meet the needs of our customers and provide a fair return to our shareholders."

Throughout the year, Capital City Bank sponsors events such as Springtime Tallahassee and Celebrate America on the Fourth of July and is an active participant in the Leon County Schools' Partners for Excellence program. Consistent financial success has enabled the bank to support a variety of local not-for-profit organizations, as well. The Capital City Group Foundation was organized in 1983 specifically to address the needs of the community regarding education, urban affairs, health, the arts, housing, and the environment.

Equally important is the service provided by dedicated Capital City directors, officers, and associates who give their time as civic leaders and volunteers. In 1989 the Julian V. Smith Community Service Award was established to recognize employees with a record of outstanding service within the community. The award is in honor of the late Julian V. Smith, a well-known Capital City banker, community leader, and humanitarian.

Despite changes that may have occurred in the bank's physical makeup, Capital City Bank has retained the fundamental values established over 100 years ago. Concern for the customer, pride in the community, good management, and a conservative approach—these are the elements that combine to make Capital City Bank more than just a bank. ◆

GTO, INC.

What began as Lester Tabb's need for a way to open his driveway gate has become the world's largest manufacturer of do-it-yourself, low voltage gate operators. Begun in 1987 as a partnership between Tabb and company president Chuck Mitchell, GTO now has over 50,000 gate operators in more than 50 countries, from the Arctic to the Amazon.

Unlike garage door openers, which are found in sheltered locations of relatively uniform size, gate openers are found on small gates, huge gates, gates made of varying types of materials, in every climate on earth, and on innumerable types of terrain and slopes. In addition, the nearest source of electricity to operate a gate may be too far for conventional electrical hook-up. By providing a low voltage battery and a solar powered charger, GTO assures its customers that wherever they have a gate, they can have a GTO operator to open, close, lock, and unlock it. Being independent of electricity is especially important in countries where electrical service is either unreliable or intermittent. Single or dual installations are available on gates from 3.5 feet to 20 feet wide and for gates weighing up to 350 pounds.

The genius of GTO's professional (The GTO Pro) and residential (The Mighty Mule and The E-Z Gate) lines of gate openers is that they are simple and inexpensive. The attractiveness of GTO as a citizen of Tallahassee is how clean the manufacturing process is and how committed the company is to the city. Zinc, steel, and plastic remnants are recycled to become raw materials. Virtually all of each operator's parts are manufactured at GTO's 35,000-square-foot facility, including all zinc die-casting, plastic injection molding, and high-speed metal stamping. Computer boards are built and stuffed, as are electrical components and connectors. All assembly, shipping, and receiving are handled out of the same facility. This highly vertical integration means that GTO is the most flexible manufacturer of swing gate operators in the world. Approximately 10 percent of GTO's shipments are exported to other countries, and the business is divided roughly 50/50 into the professional line of operators and those destined for the residential do-it-yourself market.

Almost all of GTO's employees are long-time residents of Tallahassee, which provides the company with a good pool of skilled and unskilled labor. The employment atmosphere is one of interaction among all levels, more like a family or community than a large manufacturing facility. Approximately 98 percent of the capital invested in GTO is local, too, and the return on investment for the stockholders of the privately held company has steadily increased every year.

The company has received plenty of attention for discovering and developing its market niche. In 1990, GTO received Florida's Governor's New Product Award. In 1993, *Inc.* magazine ranked GTO 120th on its list of the 500 Fastest Growing Private Companies in the United States. In 1994, GTO was a winner of the Governor's Business Leadership Award, given by the Florida Department of Commerce in recognition of the company's emphasis on quality controls and recycling efforts, as well as its significant contributions to Florida's economy and quality of life.

Finding change and product improvement a challenge and a way of doing business is a large part of GTO's corporate philosophy. The company continues to develop new types of operators and accessories for both swing gates and slide gates. With millions of gates currently manually operated around the world, the growth potential and long-term prospects for GTO are significant. GTO is well positioned to meet the challenge. ◆

GTO assures its customers that wherever they have a gate, they can have a GTO operator to open and close it by remote control.

The genius of GTO's lines of gate openers, such as The Mighty Mule, is that they are simple and inexpensive.

PROFESSIONS

◆

Tallahassee's mix of business talents and resources strengthens the professional community. Photo by Robert M. Overton.

The law firm of Macfarlane Ausley Ferguson & McMullen was formed in February 1994 by the merger of two of Florida's oldest and most prestigious law firms—Macfarlane Ferguson of Tampa and Clearwater, and Ausley, McMullen, McGehee, Carothers & Proctor of Tallahassee. The firm provides high quality legal and governmental representation to local, regional, national, and international clients. The merged firms share a corporate culture that supports the different strenghts of each, and the merger has combined the best qualities of two highly respected firms. Nathan B. Simpson, who was chairman of Macfarlane Ferguson, is the president of Macfarlane Ausley Ferguson & McMullen, while DuBose Ausley, the former president of Ausley, McMullen, McGehee, Carothers & Proctor, is chairman of the merged firm.

The new firm name is a true reflection of the history of the predecessor firms. The Tallahassee firm was founded in 1930 when Charles Saxon Ausley opened his law practice in Tallahassee. He was soon joined by Leroy Collins and by his brother John Ausley in 1935. Charles Ausley served as a municipal judge, mayor, and a state senator; and in 1954 Leroy Collins was elected governor of Florida. From this early commitment to public service, the Tallahassee firm established a strong tie to government and

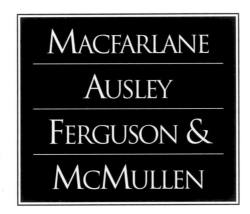

MACFARLANE AUSLEY FERGUSON & McMULLEN

developed expertise in governmental relations, supported by litigation strengths, that exists to the present time. Since its beginning, the firm has continually played a key role in shaping public policy in Florida.

The Tampa firm originated when Hugh C. Mcfarlane arrived in Tampa in 1884 to begin his legal career. He was joined by his son Howard P. Macfarlane in 1918, Cody Fowler of Oklahoma in 1924, and Chester Ferguson in 1935. Kenneth McKay, the grandson of the founder of the Lykes family business empire, was a member of the firm in the early 1900s. Lykes remains one of the firm's major clients today. The firm's legal practice was based on representing commercial interests that developed as the city of Tampa became an international port and the center of business, industry, and agriculture for the west coast of Florida.

The Clearwater firm of McMullen, Everett, Logan, Marquardt & Cline, founded in 1946 by J. Tweed McMullen, merged with Macfarlane Ferguson in 1993.

The 1994 merger combined commercial and business expertise with a broad knowledge of governmental and political relations and strong litigation skills, resulting in a staff of more than 110 lawyers, and offices in Tampa, Clearwater, and Tallahassee. The firm offers legal representation in all areas of civil law, including complex litigation and appeals, antitrust matters, administrative law, international transactions, maritime matters, environmental litigation and toxic tort litigation, environmental permitting and land use planning, eminent domain and condemnation, labor and employment law, health care law, media law, public utilities and telecommunications regulatory matters, state and federal taxation, banking, finance, probate, trusts, estates, corporate law, and commercial and residential real estate transactions.

(Left to right) John K. Aurell, Kenneth H. Hart, DuBose Ausley, James Harold Thompson, and C. Gary Williams are among the attorneys who represent clients before all agencies of state government. Photo by Robert M. Overton.

(Left to right) John P. Fons, John R. Beranek, James D. Beasley, C. Graham Carothers, and Lee L. Willis, pictured in the Lawyers' Lounge of the Florida Supreme Court, handle numerous appellate matters and represent public utility clients before the Florida Public Service Commission. Photo by Robert M. Overton.

(Left to right) William M. Smith, M. Julian Proctor Jr., Margaret B. Ausley, Timothy B. Elliott, H. Palmer Proctor, Emily S. Waugh, and Robert A. Pierce stand in front of the newly remodeled Capital City Bank building. They handle general corporate matters, trusts and estates, transactional and tax work, and regulatory matters. Photo by Robert M. Overton.

Attorneys in the firm have varied backgrounds that enhance their respective practices. Among the group are former circuit court judges, a former District Court of Appeals judge, a small claims judge, holders of advanced degrees in taxation, CPAs, former bank presidents, former general counsels for the Department of Revenue and the Department of Transportation, a National Labor Relations Board Field Attorney, an Assistant U.S. Attorney, Assistant State Attorney, law clerks to a U.S. Circuit Judge and a Florida Supreme Court Justice, General Counsel and Special Counsel to governors, and members of the Florida legislature. The firm also includes two former Speakers of the Florida House of Representatives.

The public service commitment of the founders of the firm remains a hallmark today. Attorneys in the firm serve or have served as members of the Florida Constitution Revision Commission, Florida Commission on Ethics, U.S. Circuit Judge Nominating Commission for 11th Circuit, Judicial Nominating Commission for 2nd Judicial Circuit of Florida, chair and members of the current Federal Judicial Nominating Commission, and as coordinators for U.S. District Court Naturalization ceremonies. The firm has produced three chairmen of the Florida Board of Regents, the chairman of the Florida Transportation Commission, a director of the Federal Reserve Bank of Atlanta, a president of the Florida School Board Attorneys' Association, and members and chairs of numerous state government agency committees and county and local government committees.

Attorneys in the firm hold professional memberships in the American College of Trial Lawyers, the American College of Probate Laywers, The Best Lawyers in America, the International Academy of Trial Lawyers, the National Health Lawyers Association, the Florida Hospital Association, arbitration panels, as members and chairs of many committees of the Florida Bar Association, and members of the bar associations of Georgia, Alabama, Mississippi, Ohio, North Carolina, New York, Virginia, Missouri, Pennsylvania, and Illinois. Firm members have also served on the board of

governors of the American Bar Association and as president of the Florida Bar.

Civic and community activities of firm members include serving as members, officers, directors, or volunteers in numerous organizations, including as trustees of Florida International University Foundation, Washington and Lee University, the University of Florida Law Center Association, Florida State University Foundation, Florida International University Foundation, and as adjunct professors at law schools and volunteers in law school mentor programs.

In 1989 the firm, together with 49 other law firms in or near their respective state capitals, formed the State Capital Law Firm Group. The organization enhances the firms' proficiency and enables them to better serve their clients by sharing information about the practice of law before state legislative, judicial, and executive bodies. It gives Macfarlane Ausley important contacts in all areas of the country.

Macfarlane Ausley's legal expertise, governmental knowledge, and background of dedication to quality service for its clients keep it prepared to meet the changing dynamics in business and government. The firm has excellent staff support, and the collegial atmosphere that prevails fosters a comfortable working relationship among attorneys, between attorneys and staff, and between clients and attorneys. The firm is widely known as one of the most efficiently managed and administered legal practices in the state. Full advantage is made of the latest in computerization and other office technology. Attorneys are provided with the most advanced on-line reference and research services and with a comprehensive law library.

Macfarlane Ausley is inspired by the history of its past with a dedication to continue providing competent, quality legal services to its clients in the future. The firm is proud to participate in the exciting growth of Tallahassee as the capital city moves into the twenty-first century. ◆

(Left to right) Michael J. Glazer, J. Marshall Conrad, Van P. Geeker, R. Stan Peeler, Deborah S. Minnis, and Carla A. Green handle a variety of legal issues from media and employment law to condemnation and tax matters. Photo by Robert M. Overton.

Thomas Howell Ferguson P.A. is Tallahassee's leading CPA firm and consulting practice. The strength, skills, and knowledge that come from its former affiliation with a Big Six firm are combined with deep roots in the Tallahassee area to provide fully integrated accounting, consulting, and tax services in a rapidly expanding market. For over four decades, the practice has served a broad and diverse array of prominent north Florida commercial, governmental, and not-for-profit clients in virtually every sector of the Tallahassee economy.

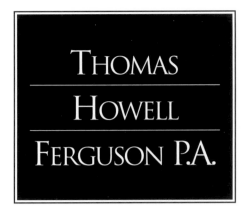

THOMAS HOWELL FERGUSON P.A.

The principals—John Perry Thomas, Winston Howell, and Bill Ferguson—are actively involved in every project, overseeing teams specifically chosen for their professionalism, skills, and specialized expertise. All three principals have national experience, yet are north Florida natives with an extraordinary commitment to their community. They see Tallahassee and the surrounding area as a vibrant market with a high degree of stability and sophisticated financial consulting needs. These professional requirements, plus the area's desirable lifestyle, attract high-caliber employees who are dedicated to addressing client needs as a team task.

In addition to traditional accounting services, Thomas Howell Ferguson maintains a significant consulting practice which provides services ranging from strategic planning and organizational consulting to a multitude of other diverse activities, including merger and acquisitions, transaction structuring, negotiations, personnel deployment, financial systems consulting, and litigation support services. Consulting and advisory services are provided as part of an integrated service philosophy that incorporates tax, auditing, and accounting services with personalized value-added services.

"To provide the highest level of personal and professional service to every client, with seasoned judgment, creativity, and responsiveness" is Thomas Howell Ferguson's mission statement. The principals—(seated) John Perry Thomas, (left to right) Bill Ferguson, and Winston Howell—are actively involved in every project the company handles.

Thomas Howell Ferguson's focus on industry specialization and its concentration of technical skills reflect the firm's commitment to building superior service capabilities that can be provided in an efficient, cost-effective manner. Major industries served by Thomas Howell Ferguson include insurance, real estate, construction, government, public finance, and tax-exempt organizations. The firm also serves a wide variety of prominent general commercial concerns throughout north Florida. Within each industry group, the firm serves a breadth of organizations varying from large publicly held corporations and public entities to privately owned businesses. For example, the Thomas Howell Ferguson insurance practice includes self insurance trusts, managed care (HMO) organizations, workers' compensation trusts, guaranty funds, and joint underwriting associations. In addition, the firm's public finance group serves state and local housing finance agencies, interlocal government finance commissions and funds, and economic development financing organizations.

Many of the firm's client relationships span a decade or more, especially in the public sector and commercial areas of its practice. Most of Thomas Howell Ferguson's clients are accustomed to the skills, services, and resources that normally are available only from national and international firms. They appreciate this same level of service, plus local market knowledge and flexibility, being available in Tallahassee through the principals' multidisciplinary training, extensive Big Six experience, and their philosophy of hiring the best talent available. In fact, in recent years two of their employees have been recipients of the Elijah Watts Sells Award, given for high distinction on the national CPA exam.

Pursuit of ever-higher standards for the profession is a hallmark of the firm. Though unique for a firm of its size, Thomas Howell Ferguson has had representatives on both the American Institute of CPAs Auditing Standards Board and the Financial Accounting Standards Advisory Council. The principals have also served on the board of directors of the American Institute of CPAs and the board of governors of the Florida Institute of CPAs.

In addition to service to the profession, the firm strongly encourages employees to serve the community in volunteer capacities. This strengthens and broadens the individual as well as provides time and talent to organizations such as the American Cancer Society, American Red Cross, the Arts Alliance, Florida Special Olympics, the Partners for Excellence program with Leon County Schools, the Tallahassee Memorial Hospital Foundation, the Chamber of Commerce, Leadership Tallahassee, and many others.

The future for Thomas Howell Ferguson lies in the expansion of specialized industry initiatives and growth that will be generated through the emphasis on personalized service and up-to-the-minute capabilities. The firm's presence in the state capital and its recognized professional expertise that goes significantly beyond traditional accounting activities are key to continued statewide recognition and the expansion of its practice base. ◆

The second largest law firm in the state of Florida, Greenberg Traurig Hoffman Lipoff Rosen & Quentel, P.A. provides its clients with practical and result-oriented strategies and solutions tailored to their individual needs. The full-service commercial law firm has offices in Miami, Fort Lauderdale, West Palm Beach, Washington, D.C., New York City, and Tallahassee. The firm's responsive approach to client service often cuts across legal subject matter, applying the right expertise and resources to provide cost-effective solutions. Greenberg Traurig represents numerous local, regional, national, and international clients ranging from Fortune 500 companies, banks and financial institutions, and insurance companies to leveraged buy-out companies, airlines, entrepreneurs, governments, other law firms, and charitable and civic organizations.

It was the 1992 merger with the Tallahassee law firm of Roberts, Baggett, LaFace, and Richard that solidified Greenberg Traurig's position as one of the most influential firms in Florida. Says Fred W. Baggett, managing shareholder of the Tallahassee office, "The goal of the Tallahassee office is to be the integral link to provide government-related services to the clients of Greenberg Traurig, which is a large, multidisciplinary national law firm."

Indeed, with offices just one block from Florida's Capitol and legislative buildings and three blocks from Florida's Supreme Court, Greenberg Traurig attorneys and clients have quick physical access to the heart of the nation's fourth largest state to accompany the ready political access provided by the shareholders of the Tallahassee office. Senior shareholders Ronald C. LaFace and Barry Richard, along with Baggett, bring more than 60 years of combined legal experience and leadership to the overall firm and to their 16-member office.

The strengths of the Tallahassee office—legislative and governmental representation, administrative and regulatory law, health care, environmental, commercial litigation and complex transactional work, all complement the strengths of Greenberg Traurig's other offices. Greenberg Traurig

maintains one of the largest municipal finance and corporate securities practices in the South. Other practice areas include appellate, complex commercial litigation, employment law, immigration law, international law, international trade, real estate law, tax law, trust and estates, alcohol beverage control, franchising, and intellectual property law.

The legal approach of the Tallahassee office of Greenberg Traurig is based on a successful practice philosophy which combines business and political discernment with legal acuity on behalf of the clients seeking a broad-based approach to their legal needs. And this is all done in a manner and style reflective of the Southern charm and grace that permeates business and government in Tallahassee. Long-standing client relationships are the norm, both between client and firm and between client and attorney, and participation in civic and community life is regarded both as an obligation and an opportunity.

The future for the Tallahassee office of Greenberg Traurig lies in expanding on the synergy between the state capital office and the resources and client base of the firm's other offices, while maintaining the personal, personable service and style that are so familiar and have been so successful. Each new relationship and chance to work with existing clients will be an opportunity to achieve positive results for the client in ways that are consistent with each client's business objectives. ◆

The Tallahassee office of Greenberg Traurig Hoffman Lipoff Rosen & Quentel, P.A. is located at the corner of College and Adams Avenues.

Since the mid-'60s Florida has experienced unparalleled growth in population and has emerged in the '90s as the fourth largest state in the nation. This growth, while affording great economic opportunities, continues to produce critical issues and challenges for business, government, and the investment community. Predominant issues of statewide importance are resolved in

MESSER, VICKERS, CAPARELLO, MADSEN, GOLDMAN & METZ, P.A.

Tallahassee, the center for state government.

Since 1968 members of the law firm of Messer, Vickers, Caparello, Madsen, Goldman and Metz, residing and working in Tallahassee, have been closely involved in the decision-making process. The firm has successfully represented regional, national, and international clients in matters pending before the Florida legislature and in judicial and administrative forums throughout the state. The firm's environmental, regulatory, and tax practices include both the State of Florida and local government agencies.

To enhance its effectiveness, the firm has developed and maintained specialized areas of practice, including the following:

- Legislative, administrative, and governmental affairs
- State and local taxation
- Corporate, commercial, and tax litigation
- Federal tax, including business and estate planning
- Insurance and health care regulation
- Land use and environmental issues
- Regulated utilities and telecommunication companies including proceedings before the Florida Public Service Commission
- Mediation

While acknowledging that the first order of professional responsibility is the effective and successful representation of clients, members of the firm strongly believe that professional responsibility includes public and community service. The firm is proud of its founding partner, Elliott Messer, whose public service has included two consecutive terms as chairman of the Tallahassee Area Chamber of Commerce, membership on the Florida Constitution Revision Commission, the Governor's Education Commission, the State Commission on Private

Members of the law firm of Messer, Vickers, Caparello, Madsen, Goldman and Metz continue to search for and find contemporary solutions to problems facing the firm's private and public clients. Pictured are (left to right) Dominic M. Caparello, Cass D. Vickers, James Elliott Messer, Suzanne Mann, and Robert S. Goldman. Photo by Robert M. Overton.

Property Rights, the Telecommunications Tax Commission, and the boards of the Florida Chamber of Commerce and Florida Tax Watch.

For Cass Vickers and Bob Goldman, community service has included leadership in the resolution of major tax issues through the Florida Chamber of Commerce and the nationally based Institute of Property Taxation. Cass has served on the State Sales Tax Study Commission and the board of the Florida Chamber, and Bob has served on the board of the Institute.

Dom Caperello has served as president of the Tallahassee Bar Association and chairman of the Judicial Nominating Commission for the Second Judicial Circuit. Mike Madsen is a current member of the Tallahassee-Leon County Planning Commission, and Steve Metz is presently serving as chairman of the Florida Chamber's Task Force on Crime. Of primary importance to the Task Force on Crime is the search for a solution to juvenile delinquency and the commission of violent crime.

Members of the law firm of Messer, Vickers, Caparello, Madsen, Goldman and Metz will continue to search for and find contemporary solutions to problems facing the firm's private and public clients. Of equal importance, firm members will stay involved in public and community service.

Florida is a dynamic state with abundant natural resources, a multicultural diversity, and an exciting economic future. Tallahassee is a beautiful city, the center of state government, the residence of the Florida Supreme Court, and the First District Court of Appeals, the location of two major universities, and the site of the National High Magnetic Laboratory. In so many ways, Messer-Vickers has been a part of it all and is proud to have been so. ◆

Members of the firm are proud of their association with Tallahassee. Shown (first row) are H. Michael Madsen, Floyd R. Self, Stephen W. Metz, (second row) Timothy J. Warfel, and Lauchlin T. Waldoch. Photo by Robert M. Overton.

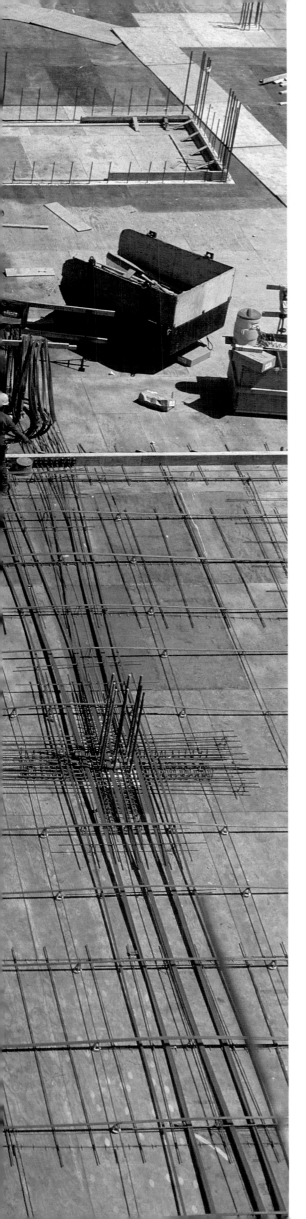

REAL ESTATE &
CONSTRUCTION

*From concept to completion, Tallahassee's building and real estate
industry shapes tomorrow's skyline and neighborhoods.
Photo by Robert M. Overton.*

For more than 50 years, Watkins Engineers & Constructors has led the way in industrial process design and construction services in the Southeast. Over time, the quality and excellence associated with the Watkins' name have made the company a major player among the nation's most sophisticated industrial, process, and commercial engineers and constructors.

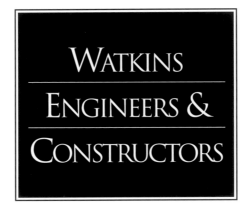

WATKINS ENGINEERS & CONSTRUCTORS

E. M. Watkins & Company was formed in 1944 by Buck Watkins to provide design and construction services to north Florida and Alabama's emerging wood products and pulp and paper industries. Early client relationships have forged remark-

E. M. Watkins & Company was formed in 1944 by Buck Watkins to provide design and construction services to north Florida and Alabama's emerging wood products and pulp and paper industries.

able client/company partnerships, as, over time, Watkins has been retained for the long term to provide mainte-nance and retrofit services for plants once they were operative. For example, after the Buckeye pulp mill in Perry, Florida, started up in 1954, Watkins successfully bid a small project at the plant. Forty years later Watkins is still meeting the design and construction requirements for Buckeye on a full-time basis. There are Watkins employees who worked 30 years there without missing a paycheck. Offspring from these original employees form the nucleus of Watkins' field force today.

This unusual employee longevity in an industry known for chronic turnover comes about because Watkins approaches the business differently. The company assumes, going into a contract, that they will be with the cus-tomer for the long haul. This is communicated and proven, time and time again, to Watkins' employees, who find a uniquely stable working environment. They, in turn, reward Watkins with their loyalty, allowing Watkins to make promises of service delivery that are met every time. As a result, Watkins is the largest employer of hourly craft workers in the region, employing, on the average, more than 1,500 pipe fitters, boilermakers, millwrights, electricians, ironworkers, carpenters, and laborers. This is in addition to a management, engineering, and administrative staff of over 400.

For more than 50 years, Watkins Engineers & Constructors has led the way in industrial process design and construction services in the Southeast with projects such as the BDM Office Building in Huntsville, Alabama.

Given this promise of performance, Watkins' clients expect quality, and they should know it when they see it. They are the giants of industry: Procter & Gamble, Buckeye, Air Products & Chemicals, E.I. Dupont, Occidental Chemical, Georgia-Pacific, Stone Container, Weyerhaeuser, International Paper, and Cargill. How a local Tallahassee firm became a national and internationally known concern speaks to the area's quality of life. It attracted Dorothy Watkins, as her husband went off to war, and the city's livability has kept the company headquar-ters here ever since. As the company grew, its central location between Pensacola, Jacksonville, and Perry, Florida, and central Georgia was ideal.

The industrial areas in which Watkins is a leader include design and construction of huge processing plants, from pulp and paper, its beginnings, to chemicals, mining, cement, food processing, and beverages. Many a synthetic detergent plant in the United States has been built and maintained by Watkins, including plants in Alexandria, Louisiana, Augusta, Georgia, and Sacramento, California.

The firm's capabilities and reputation in design and mechan-ical process installations in the Southeast made it a natural companion for one of the world's largest constructors. Watkins was acquired in 1983 by San Francisco-based Dillingham Construction Corporation, a world-renowned heavy, industrial, and commercial contractor. As a wholly owned subsidiary, Watkins operates autonomously. Satellite offices are located in Jacksonville and Pensacola, Florida, Columbia and Greenville, South Carolina, and Mount Arlington, New Jersey. These national locations enhance Watkins' ability to provide quick response to customer requirements, creating the long-term relationships for which the company is widely known.

Given a promise of performance, Watkins' clients expect quality, and they should know it when they see it. They are the industry giants like Georgia-Pacific.

power and pulp and paper industries, and lime kilns, including one of the largest ones in the world, for cement, rock product, and pulp and paper companies. One of the most challenging environmental projects Watkins undertook was the laying of a 96-inch diameter pipe under a river to connect a 120-acre aeration lagoon to a pulp mill in Taylor County, Florida.

These projects are accomplished through the skills of the employees utilizing state-of-the-art technology and methods, and through excellent, ongoing communications with the customer. Computer-assisted designs now replace the superb, hand-drawn renderings of the past. Watkins is a large employer of the graduates of the joint FSU/FAMU Engineering School, known for producing outstanding minority engineers. Says Don Sundgren, president: "The company is unique among firms its size for its emphasis and sophistication in both engineering and construction, which keeps us on the technical edge of cost management, computers, and design/build technology." Together with craft people and administrative staff, some 3 million effort hours per year contribute towards a $60-million Watkins' payroll. The impact of this firm on Tallahassee is powerful, and the company is a good corporate citizen, participating in the Chamber of Commerce and numerous civic affairs.

For example, Watkins has provided on-site design and construction services for Weyerhaeuser's Oglethorpe, Georgia, pulp mill since it started up in 1980, and for Cargill's Frostproof, Florida, citrus processing plant since 1981. Watkins built a synthetic detergent plant for Procter & Gamble in Alexandria, Louisiana, in 1968 and is still on-site there as well. The New Jersey office represents Watkins' move into the bulk material handling business, a natural adjunct to its emphasis on processes.

Watkins' commercial division has been a major player in the local construction market, too, building such projects as the Florida State University Business School, Undergraduate Physics Lab, School of Library Science, and a 1,000-space parking garage. The Florida Agricultural and Mechanical University School of Nursing, the Ramada Inn North, and the Associated Industries of Florida headquarters building bear the Watkins' imprint, as does the Leon County Justice Complex, the Woodcrest Atrium Building, and the state government Satellite Office Complex. Regionally, Watkins built the Bay Medical Center in Panama City, Florida, and multiple high profile projects in Huntsville, Alabama, and Jacksonville, Florida. Watkins' engineering and industrial divisions worked together to convert the Seminole Kraft Linerboard Mill in Jacksonville from a virgin timber mill to the largest 100 percent recycled fiber mill in the world, processing 1,200 tons per day.

As commercial and industrial concerns have turned towards protecting the environment, Watkins' skills and expertise have been called upon to build, modify, maintain, and repair air and water quality systems such as electrostatic precipitators in the

Watkins built a synthetic detergent plant for Procter & Gamble in Alexandria, Louisiana, in 1968 and is still on-site there today.

Echoing its past, Watkins Engineers & Constructors expects to maintain and surpass its present position among the leading national and international engineering and construction firms. Growth will come through internal expansion and the studied acquisition of companies with similar capabilities in different markets, both by industry and location.

According to Sundgren, "Our success depends on providing a quality of service and value which exceeds our client's expectations." Ernest Watkins Jr., son of the founder, says, "The greatest reward is additional work that comes from existing clients. Then you know you've done your best, and that they know it." So it is that a home-grown company that has become a national presence from a town the size of Tallahassee is poised for the future on a solid foundation of proud tradition, progressive practices, and excellent service. ◆

Since 1906, customers have expected the best from Coldwell Banker, and since 1982 in Tallahassee, they have had their expectations exceeded with Hartung and Associates Inc., Realtors.

Selected in 1981 as the only Coldwell Banker affiliate in the Tallahassee area, Hartung and Associates maintain quality customer relationships by hiring only full-time, professional real estate agents. The training, knowledge, and sales and marketing tools provided by Coldwell Banker serve to enhance the high expectations president and owner Chip Hartung and vice president and general manager Kitty D'Amico have of their sales agents. Many of their professionals have been with the firm more than five years, some since the firm began.

COLDWELL BANKER HARTUNG AND ASSOCIATES INC., REALTORS

The affiliation with Coldwell Banker came about because of strongly compatible business philosophies between the national firm and Chip Hartung. Providing the most professional and ethical real estate services possible to its clients and customers is the mission statement of Hartung and Associates. Coldwell Bankers philosophy of superior customer satisfaction and Hartung's mission were a natural match.

To encourage this philosophy among its agents, Hartung and Associates provides awards for customer service that are more coveted than the more widely recognized production designations offered by most other real estate firms. In fact, Hartung's customer service award was in place before Coldwell Banker began offering a similar award nationally, an example of the close points of view and cutting-edge approach Hartung and Associates takes.

The success of this approach is unmistakable. Hartung and Associates now have Tallahassee's largest market share. But in keeping with their customer satisfaction approach, customers only know they are receiving excellent service and personal attention to the last detail. "Our agents practice our business philosophy day in and day out," says Chip Hartung. In a perpetuating cycle, providing the best possible service with integrity and attention to a customer's needs leads to quality service, which generates high expectations, which leads to customer satisfaction.

As a result, team spirit among Hartung's associates is unique, as is the professionalism that has led several of the firm's members to be in the top one or two percent of Coldwell Banker's 50,000 international associates year in and year out. This level of production and customer service has made Hartung and Associates one of the top 100 offices in the Coldwell Banker international company.

Hartung's business philosophy spreads to its community profile, too. Both Hartung and D'Amico have served on the major local real estate industry boards and Chamber of Commerce. Hartung has served as president of the Tallahassee Board of Realtors and D'Amico as vice president. Hartung also served as district vice president of the Florida Association of Realtors. They have also participated on local human service boards such as the YMCA, Big Brothers, and United Way along with Coldwell Banker National Habitat for Humanity.

Coldwell Banker Hartung and Associates Inc. is committed to Tallahassee. It is with an attitude of caring and respect, and a desire to provide its citizens the most basic human need of shelter that continue to drive Hartung and Associates to be the best. ◆

The corporate offices of Coldwell Banker Hartung and Associates Inc., Realtors are located at 3303 Thomasville Road. Photo by Jeb MacVittie.

The training, knowledge, and sales and marketing tools provided by Coldwell Banker serve to enhance the high expectations vice president and general manager Kitty D'Amico and president and owner Chip Hartung have of their sales agents.

This continuity and knowledge of the market mean that Hartung and Associates provides their customers with unequaled expertise in all types of residential and commercial real estate and property management. They serve all types of markets in the Tallahassee area, from student housing to high-end residential, from small retail to large commercial. In addition, Hartung and Associates represents buyers and sellers in national relocation programs and many of Tallahassee's premier builders.

Since its beginnings in 1973 as a general contractor, Sperry and Associates has concentrated on bringing one product to their customers—service. Pre-engineered steel buildings and metal roofs are the firm's specialty, and they concentrate on commercial and low-rise construction. Other interests include office and retail renovation.

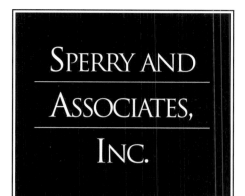

The firm's client list is a "Who's Who" of business and industry in Tallahassee, north Florida, south Georgia, and the nation. Some of Sperry and Associates' more dramatic projects include a 32,000-square-foot manufacturing addition for Stanadyne Automotive, Inc.; a 54,000-square-foot remodeling

The Capital Eye Center, constructed by Sperry and Associates in Tallahassee, is a 10,000-square-foot eye care center with 3,000 square feet of H.R.S. approved surgical facilities.

job for the Capital Outlet Center that involved three levels of government as well as the client; a complete structural renovation and expansion that doubled the size of Capital City Bank's South Monroe Street branch while the bank remained open; and a 100,000-square-foot facility built for The Printing House. Recently, Sperry and Associates have put the roofs on a number of aging school buildings in rural counties surrounding Tallahassee. These maintenance-free, 20-year weather tight warrantied roofs save the school districts' taxpayers money due to longer life cycle, reduced utilities, and negligible maintenance costs.

The secret to the outstanding levels of quality and service at Sperry is the "design-build" concept. This means that the firm works with a customer from concept to completion. By getting to know the customer's needs so completely, and having highly skilled and knowledgeable employees familiar with all phases of each project, Sperry and Associates can tailor every solution to every building problem individually. In addition, all of the steel and concrete craftsmen work in-house. This work force stability assures customers of on-time project completion, especially critical to commercial clients and those who

continue to operate during metal-roof retrofits.

Such is Sperry's reputation that it rarely bids on projects, but is a marketing-based contractor. The result of this attention to need and detail and commitment to service is nothing short of astonishing. Given the north Florida/south Georgia market area, Sperry is one of American Buildings Company's smaller markets. Yet America's third-largest supplier of pre-engineered metal buildings and roofs has listed Sperry and Associates among its top 20 producers every year since 1980. Annually, Sperry wins 2 or 3 of 50 national building design awards from ABC as well as roofing and architectural awards and retrofit awards. In 1984, the company had the high honor of receiving the first national Nobilis Aquila (President's Award) from ABC, and in 1993, was its Roofer of the Year.

With such heady results, the company is remarkably down home. In fact, it recently became partially employee-owned through an employee stock option plan. The company's officers are Todd Sperry, son of Don and Jane Sperry, the founders of Sperry and Associates, and their sons-in-law, Tony Benton and Bart Wells. As long-time residents of the Tallahassee area, all are involved in community and civic organizations and activities from the Chamber of Commerce to the Coalition for Positive Growth Management to trade organizations such as the Association of Builders and Contractors and the Tallahassee Builders Association.

The future for Sperry and Associates looks much like its past—steady, controlled growth that comes from providing a superior product with the best in customer service and quality workmanship, from start to finish, in a well-defined market niche that is growing in demand. ◆

Sperry and Associates tailors every solution to every building problem individually. A prime example of this dedication to service is Comcast Cable's 16,000-square-foot office, studio, and vehicle storage building.

Mention integrity in the real estate industry in Tallahassee and Noblin Realty invariably crops up. Mention thriving residential developments that have housed thousands of Tallahasseeans and were so visionary and well conceived that they became templates for many other subdivisions, and you hear Millard Noblin's name again.

NOBLIN REALTY

Known for his dedication to improving the professional standards of his field, his astute business sense, environmental awareness, and a devotion to many community organizations, Noblin is a native Tallahasseean and Florida State University graduate. In 1971 he created Millard J. Noblin Realty, Inc., an independently owned real estate brokerage company specializing in residential real estate that unerringly reflects the characteristics of its founder.

Millard J. Noblin, president and Ann Brockett, vice president and managing broker of Noblin Realty, keep agents at their best and assures that customers and clients receive the finest service available in the Tallahassee residential market.

The goal of Noblin Realty is to pursue a certain purpose in the community—one of integrity, high quality service for customers and clients, honesty, and fairness. Aiming high has brought Noblin Realty the enviable growth rate of between 16 to 30 percent per year in closed residential volume. Recent years have seen total transactions at Noblin Realty exceeding 1,500 per year, with the average annu-al closed volume per agent at over $2.8 million.

Such results are largely due to Noblin's commitment to hire only full-time, high-caliber agents. These highly qualified people must be very service-oriented, because even though they are independent contractors, the firm's reputation demands the best in customer service and satisfaction. Low turnover and long-term associations are strong indicators of Noblin Realty's commitment to its agents and to its customers, as is its adoption of the National Association of Realtors' ethics code as the firm's own standard.

The company's unique training program, developed and provided in-house by Ann Brockett, Noblin's vice president and managing broker, keeps agents at their best and assures that customers and clients receive the best information, advice, and service available in the Tallahassee residential market. The administrative staff compliments the team effort and supportive atmosphere that permeates every transaction at Noblin Realty, from listing to selling to consulting.

Clearly an expert in the Tallahassee residential real estate market, if not one of its most important shapers, Noblin Realty also enjoys association with the All Points Relocation Service Corporation. This service gives those who must leave the area as much assistance as possible, and provides newcomers to Tallahassee with the finest in relocation advice. Another area of leadership is in the provision of affordable housing for first-time home buyers, although Noblin is equally well-known for move-up and upscale developments.

Since 1965 Millard Noblin's vision has made a strong impact on development in Tallahassee's residential market and the northeast quadrant of the city. In 1976, implementing his vision of the future again, Noblin created the Community Realty Group, an umbrella corporation that provides support for several broker members, allowing them to share marketing ideas and buy in bulk, especially media advertising. In another visionary move, he helped found the Apalachee Land Conservancy, so becoming one of the first people in Tallahassee to recognize and appreciate the inexorable link between attractive properties, environmental sensitivity, and sound business practice.

Whatever the future holds for Noblin Realty, it will be intimately intertwined with Tallahassee's future, for Millard Noblin says, "I wouldn't live anywhere else on earth." ◆

Created in 1971, Noblin Realty, Inc. is an independently owned real estate brokerage company specializing in residential real estate.

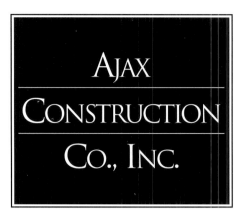

Ajax Construction, founded in 1958 by Block Smith, is a family-owned business which has served the construction needs of the north Florida and south Georgia region for the past three decades. Through the years Ajax has established a solid reputation and built a satisfied customer base by maintaining the highest professional standards.

Long a leader in constructing larger, commercial projects, Ajax is also recognized for its management of minor projects (projects of less than $500,000) and historical renovations.

Ajax Construction is a family-owned business which has served the construction needs of the north Florida and south Georgia region for the past three decades. Pictured (left to right) Doug, Block, and Kevin Smith are dedicated to a simple philosophy: "Quality Builds its Own Reputation."

Ajax's list of completed projects includes several office buildings, correctional facilities, medical facilities, industrial facilities, hotels, residential projects, and projects with historical significance.

With each project, Ajax has worked hard to build something equally important as the finished product—a strong, solid reputation: A reputation for quality building and attention to detail; a reputation for on-time, on-budget, award-winning projects; a reputation for tackling tough historical restoration projects with beautiful results; a reputation that keeps clients coming back again and again.

From the outset, Ajax Construction prefers to join the team at project initiation, providing preconstruction services during the design phase. Depending on requirements, Ajax can serve as the construction manager, as the general contractor, as a design-build contractor, or serve as a consultant providing comprehensive program management services for capital improvement programs.

At Ajax Construction, operations is broken down into two divisions: the Major Projects Division (projects in excess of $1 million) and the Minor Projects Division (projects up to $1 million). This categorizing of projects by size and scope ensures that each job receives expert direction from a

At 202,000 square feet, the National High Magnetic Lab houses one of the world's largest magnetic installations.

professional intimately familiar with the demands and requirements of that particular project. Additionally, both divisions are fully supported by the estimating, resources, controls, and accounting departments committed to client satisfaction.

This means of operation has proven successful and has provided Ajax with the knowledge and expertise to undertake a variety of projects ranging from the renovation of historical landmarks (the Columns at the Tallahassee Chamber of Commerce, the Knott House, the Bloxham House, etc.) to the completion of much larger projects (such as the $38.8 million Leon County Detention Facility). Because of Ajax's willingness to accept any challenge, the company has become noted for its innovative techniques and expertise in various methods of construction. Many projects, such as high-tech facilities, have required special features ranging from computerized graphic panels to touchscreen installations.

Ajax is a leader is other ways, too. Well before regulations required it, Ajax maintained steadfast relationships with area minority businesses and contractors. In fact, Ajax created a Minority Development Task Force whose sole purpose is to maximize minority participation on each and every project. Mirroring the company's family roots, the firm also sponsors scholarships at local universities and participates in area Chamber and Springtime Tallahassee activities.

Ajax Construction is one of Leon County's largest and most active employers, providing professional and technical positions throughout the area. Ajax Construction has the most stable workforce in the region—a workforce dedicated to the delivery of services with unsurpassed quality. And why this phenomenal success? The Ajax philosophy is simple: "Quality Builds its Own Reputation." ◆

MORGAN ELECTRIC

From its beginning, Morgan Electric has been Tallahassee's leader in quality electrical design, engineering, and construction. The company's business philosophy is to do the job right, at a fair price, on time. Over the years, Morgan Electric has done this so successfully, word-of-mouth and repeat business is all the advertising the company needs.

The company was founded in 1960 by Paul H. Morgan Sr., a master electrician. Paul H. Morgan Jr. joined the firm in 1960 at the age of 24 and began running the office side of the firm, while Paul Sr. (who retired in 1974) was out in the field. Also a master electrician, Paul Jr.'s degree in electrical engineering allowed him to guide the firm into the growing field of design/build projects.

From the mid-'60s to late '70s, Morgan Electric grew phenomenally as large construction projects demanded the design and build expertise of the company. Having the capacity to assist customers with the design of their processes as well as their buildings gave Morgan Electric the opportunity to work on unique specialty projects. These included doing all of the power and process control wiring for the Tom's Food plant in Perry, Florida; a fire suppression system for the crushed pellet fuel system at the State Hospital in Chattahoochee, Florida; and the Winewood Office Complex in Tallahassee, among others.

Forgoing the allure of becoming a large, impartial company, Morgan Electric has, since the 1980s, chosen to remain a smaller firm with an emphasis on quality, integrity, and fair prices. The company's emphasis in the '90s is on unique specialty projects in commercial construction.

The way Morgan has chosen to manage the company reflects an extension of this philosophy. Morgan Electric's foremen operate autonomously, almost as if they were independent businessmen. They have the authority to accept jobs and seek new business. Each electrician reports to a single foreman, giving a sense of teamwork and creating a remarkably stable work force; most of the foremen and many of the electricians have been with Morgan Electric for many years. Customers call on Morgan Electric because they know there is a core group of craftsmen available to do quality work reliably, backed up by an efficient, knowledgeable office staff.

It's not all work at Morgan Electric, though. The company is located in the shadow of Campbell Stadium, home of the Florida State Seminoles, 1993 NCAA National Football Champions. Certain Tallahassee families have parked on Morgan's property surrounding the company buildings for years, and tailgate parties make for festive Saturdays.

Even though Morgan Electric has the feel of a family-owned, old-fashioned company, it has been a leader in staying abreast of technological change, from being one of the first companies in Tallahassee to become computerized in its business operations, to keeping the employees fully trained on the latest in electrical technology. For example, Morgan Electric had what it takes to wire the new press and conveyor system for the *Tallahassee Democrat*, and performed all of the wiring and hook-up for defense contractor Tadiran's electrical services and equipment.

Morgan has accepted two appointments (1979-1980 and 1986-1990) to the state of Florida's Electrical Contractors Licensing Board, serving as chairman in 1989-1990.

This judicious blend of old and new has made Morgan Electric the most established and continuously operating electrical contracting business in North Florida. For Morgan Electric, the first 35 years, celebrated in February 1995, are just a harbinger of what's to come. ◆

Morgan Electric is a leader in staying abreast of technological change. For example, Morgan Electric had what it takes to wire the new press and conveyor system for the Tallahassee Democrat.

Having the capacity to assist customers with the design of their processes as well as their buildings gave Morgan Electric the opportunity to work on unique specialty projects such as the power and process control wiring for the Tom's Food plant in Perry, Florida.

FLORIDA COASTAL PROPERTIES, INC.

One of Tallahassee's charms is its close proximity to the Gulf of Mexico, and no one knows this better than Ted and Thelma Gaupin, owners of Florida Coastal Properties, Inc. Since 1973, Florida Coastal has been the premiere coastal and resort sales development and rental management company in the Big Bend area. A full-service real estate firm, the company has offices at Shell Point Beach, Crawfordville, and Carrabelle. For years, Florida Coastal has been a Wakulla County member of Tallahassee Board of Realtors Multiple Listing Service. Through the years, the company's vision and stability have made it and kept it one of the area's finest real estate firms.

The pride of Florida Coastal Properties, Inc. is the developments at Shell Point Beach, the largest pleasure mooring port between Panama City and Tampa and the first beach south of Tallahassee, 29 miles from the capital. The Gaupins' first venture in the area was Marsh Harbor Marina. They then began developing Snug Harbour, located between the Gulf and Saint Marks Wildlife Refuge. Wildlife such as eagles, osprey, bobcats, boar, and deer are regularly seen by the 400-plus year-round residents. Porpoises and manatees swim in the rivers and bays, and the fishing is some of the finest around, offering red fish, mangrove snapper, and scallops near shore and grouper, tarpon, and snapper offshore.

Through the years, the company's vision and stability have made it and kept it one of the area's finest real estate firms. Pictured here is the senior sales staff of Florida Coastal Properties: (left to right) Thelma Gaupin, Ken Voland, Carol Williams, and Ted Gaupin.

A quick 35 minutes from downtown Tallahassee are the residences at Snug Harbour, which include everything from exclusive waterfront homes to resort town-homes, studio apartments, and Victorian-style pastel homes. Paved roads, underground utilities, and concrete seawalls in the developments of Florida Coastal Properties give residents good access and unobstructed views of the Saint Marks Wildlife Refuge and the Gulf. The security gate, a feature of most Florida Coastal's developments, assures privacy, safety, and tranquility year-round. Local restaurants, the marinas, and small shops make Shell Point Beach a community unto itself.

Just across the street from Florida Coastal's Shell Point Beach office is one of the company's newest developments, Cedar Island, planned for estate homes on one-and-a-half to two-acre lots. Nearby, the Island Club development offers conventional homes with deep water access to Snug Harbour Inlet. Twenty minutes from Tallahassee, Florida Coastal is marketing River Plantation Estates on the Wakulla River. The Gaupins have recently invested in the 225-acre Wildwood Country Club, bringing an 18-hole golf course within 10 minutes of Shell Point Beach. The company's interest in the future of the communities it has developed and lives among has led to the development of Opportunity Park, a 240-acre commercial and industrial park located south of Woodville, about 15 miles and minutes south of Tallahassee.

The pride of Florida Coastal Properties is the developments at Shell Point Beach, the largest pleasure mooring port between Panama City and Tampa and the first beach south of Tallahassee.

In a coastal resort, what could be more natural than corporate support for the community that involves boating, golf, and nature trails? Each year, Florida Coastal Properties, Inc. is one of the sponsors of the Stephen C. Smith Regatta, an annual fund-raiser for the American Cancer Society at Shell Point Beach. The location of the Apalachee Bay Yacht Club at Shell Point Beach provides boating enthusiasts the facilities to enjoy the area's waterways, yacht racing, and a laid-back lifestyle.

The visions that the Gaupins and Florida Coastal Properties, Inc. have brought to Shell Point Beach and other parts of the Big Bend coast include elevated building codes and the encouragement of orderly developments, the advocacy of homeowners' associations, and the assurance that homeowners will only experience the good life in a property that appreciates in value as they enjoy the offshore breezes, gorgeous views, and close proximity to some of the most pristine waters and wildlife areas in north Florida. ◆

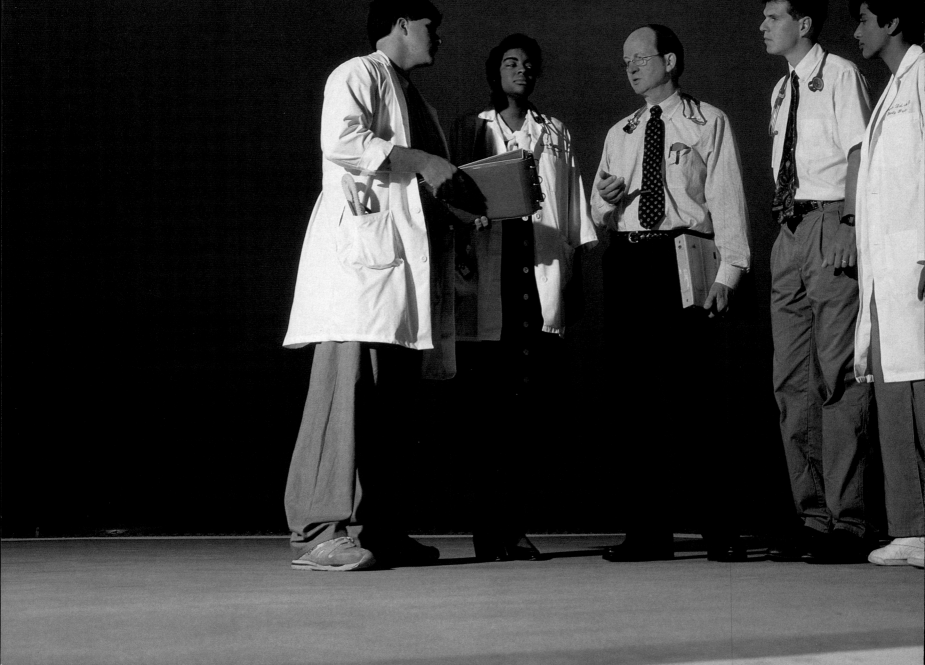

EDUCATION &
HEALTH CARE

◆

*Tallahassee's extensive health care system provides the best in
comprehensive care, complementing the area's quality of life.
Photo by Ray Stanyard.*

SCIENCE AND TECHNOLOGY AT FLORIDA STATE UNIVERSITY

I n 1997 Florida State University will celebrate the 50th anniversary of its transition from a liberal arts college for women to a coeducational university. Founded in 1857, the institution has grown in the past four decades to become one of the nation's top research universities with diverse offerings in graduate education and with exceptional strengths in scientific research.

The second oldest member (behind the University of Florida in Gainesville) of Florida's State University System, Florida State attracts nearly 30,000 students annually. Of this number, roughly 6,000 graduate students pursue advanced degrees associated with 95 masters and 65 doctorate programs.

Basic research—inquiry into the fundamental whys and hows of natural processes underlying the so-called pure sciences of biology, chemistry, math, and physics—remains a key element in Florida State's scientific mission. As a measure of its success in pursuing this charge, in 1994 FSU was named a Research University I by the Carnegie Foundation. The distinction signals Florida State's arrival in the inner circle of the nation's elite centers for higher learning, graduate training, and research.

Since the mid-1960s, campus research has experienced dramatic growth. Space devoted to research and instruction has more than doubled. Annual expenditures for externally supported research jumped from around $15 million in 1969 to $85 million in 1994. As a consequence, the campus now boasts some laboratory facilities that in overall quality and capability are without equals in the Southeast.

A prototype jet nozzle designed by fluid dynamic engineers at FSU is tested in a special lab on campus. Photo by Ray Stanyard, FSU Office of Research.

A MISSION IN MAGNETS

The newest of these facilities officially opened its doors in October 1994. Vice President Al Gore officiated at the dedication that month of the new National High Magnetic Field Laboratory, with headquarters based at Innovation Park, a research park near central campus.

Begun in 1990 by $120 million in start-up grants from the National Science Foundation and support from the State of Florida, the NHMFL is the nation's newest national laboratory. Although based at FSU, the lab is a joint collaboration between Florida State, the University of Florida, and Los Alamos National Laboratory in New Mexico.

The lab's mission is to become the world's leading center for developing and exploiting technologies in high-field magnetism, among the most intriguing research avenues at the forefront of science. Some of the world's best talents in magnet design, materials science, and theoretical physics have been drawn to Tallahassee to help launch this enterprise, which holds enormous potential for all walks of science and technology.

By late fall 1994, the lab's construction phase was all but complete, and its scientific phase was well under way. In June of that year, the lab successfully tested its first magnet that was designed and built entirely by lab scientists and engineers. The device set a new world record in its class for magnetic strength, developing a sustained field roughly 600,000 times stronger than Earth's own magnetic field. By 1997 the lab plans to have a magnet twice that powerful in operation.

High-field magnets already have become commonplace in at least one commercial field—medicine. The technology known as magnetic resonance imaging, or MRI, has now become a medical diagnostic procedure that is as common as the X-ray. At the heart of MRI technology are high magnetic fields generated by one of several types of super-strong magnets similar to those that NHMFL scientists are now developing.

Fundamental research at the lab will focus not only on how magnets can be made more powerful, but also on how this power can be put to good use in other areas of science and industry. A primary goal is unraveling the secrets of superconductivity, the phenomenon of electricity passing through a conductor without losing any energy to resistance. Superconductivity is now possible only by immersing conductors in super-cold baths of liquid helium or nitrogen. The challenge to scientists is to create room-temperature superconductivity, a phenomenon that may come about through discoveries of new materials created through the use of high magnetic fields.

GATEWAY TO BIG-TIME COMPUTING

The federal government's decision in 1990 to place the future of magnet technology in the hands of Florida State University was based largely on experience in FSU's scientific capabilities elsewhere. For example, 1994 marked the 10th

The R/V Seminole leaves port at FSU's Marine Laboratory in Franklin County, headed for a research project in the Gulf of Mexico. Photo by Ray Stanyard, FSU Office of Research.

Large-scale supercomputing, using machines with massively parallel architectures, is a focus of FSU's Supercomputer Computations Research Institute. Photo by Ray Stanyard, FSU Office of Research.

anniversary of the establishment of the Supercomputer Computations Research Institute (SCRI), launched in 1984 by a $100-million grant from the United States Department of Energy.

SCRI grew out of a national imperative to strengthen America's credentials in advanced computing technologies, which 10 years ago were in danger of being eclipsed by developments in Europe and Japan. Today, so-called "high-end" computing—that involving the most sophisticated applications and technologies—is being increasingly recognized once again as an American product, thanks in large part to federally subsidized research centers such as SCRI.

Most recently, SCRI scientists and software engineers have excelled in the area of distributed computing, so-called for its inherent mission of distributing high-end computing power to a large number of users. SCRI has become one of the nation's largest innovators of distributing computer concepts which are helping shape the way tomorrow's large-scale supercomputing in science and industry will be done.

SCRI itself is a direct outgrowth of two traditional FSU strengths that have largely characterized the university's emergence as a major research institute. Since 1957 Florida State has been the home of a high-energy particle physics program that today enjoys a world-class reputation. For nearly 40 years, these physicists have been involved in large, international collaborations focusing on investigations into the fundamental constituents of matter.

Relying heavily as it does on advanced computing, in this sense such work is similar to other strong campus research programs, notably in such fields as meteorology,

oceanography, chemistry, math, and statistics. With its emphasis on solving intensely complicated problems in the physical sciences, SCRI acquired and developed strengths in advanced supercomputing as a natural progression of FSU's computing capabilities which, since 1965, have been unrivaled in the Southeast.

FROM EARTH TO EARTHLINGS

Putting high-powered computers in the hands of campus scientists has paid off elsewhere. For many years now, meteorology has been largely a computer-driven field. Not coincidentally, Florida State's Department of Meteorology is recognized as one of the country's finest. The department's stellar faculty includes some of the world's leading experts in large-scale weather (computer) modeling and in remote weather analysis using satellite telemetry and Doppler radar techniques. FSU-designed computer models of hurricane behavior and the phenomenon known as El Niño—the periodic over-warming of the southern Pacific Ocean—are now in use the world over, and often in academic and government units run by FSU-trained meteorologists.

Cancer research at Florida State focuses on exploiting what often are subtle differences between normal cells and cancer cells. Photo by Ray Stanyard, FSU Office of Research.

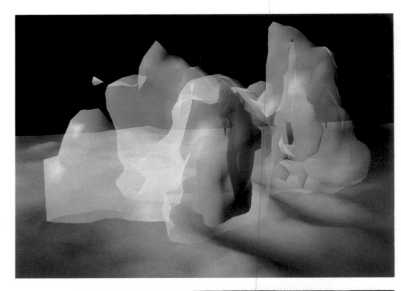

Florida State is a world leader in the computer modeling of large, complex weather systems. The image is an FSU computerized depiction of data collected by three Doppler radars trained on a real thunderstorm. Photo by Ray Stanyard, FSU Office of Research.

Life sciences research, although not traditionally computer-intensive, is becoming more so of late. By themselves, though, computers aren't likely ever to be able to replace the kinds of experimental, physiological research that has led to so many of today's "medical miracles." For nearly four decades, Florida State has been an integral source of fundamental information on the physiology of neurological pathways governing growth, reproduction, and the senses of sight, taste, smell, and hearing. The University's Program in Neuroscience, made up of biologists, chemists, and psychologists, is unique to the Florida system, offering the only Ph.D. in the field of neuroscience in the state. In 1991 a $5-million Biomedical Research Facility built on main campus became the central lab for the program's members as well as other life sciences researchers on campus. This state-of-the-art facility has few peers, even on campuses with medical schools.

NUCLEAR POWER TO LEARNING POWER

The coming-on-line of the NHMFL, with its Florida State headquarters, has helped focus renewed attention on several other FSU strengths. Among those programs already enjoying national and international reputations are the following:

• The Nuclear Research Program—Begun in the late 1950s, this program now boasts the most powerful nuclear accelerator outside of a government lab in the South. A $3.6-million upgrade of the university's Tandem Van De Graaf nuclear accelerator in 1986 funded installation of a 60-foot-long superconducting linear accelerator, which doubled the energy of ion beams generated by the Tandem. The higher energy levels put FSU's nuclear research capabilities on par with those of some of the nation's best nuclear research centers.

• The FAMU/FSU Fluid Mechanics Research Laboratory— This program is an outgrowth of the FAMU/FSU College of Engineering, begun in 1984. Experts in applied math, computational and experimental fluid dynamics, acoustics, and robotics come together in this program that now ranks in the top five fluid mechanics research centers in the nation. Each year the lab attracts nearly $1 million annually in support from aerospace contractors and government agencies seeking better designs in jet engines and noise control.

• The Center for Materials Research and Technology (MARTECH)–Established in 1985, this program combines FSU's interdisciplinary strengths in physics, engineering, and chemistry on problems inhibiting advancement in

An FSU researcher adjusts a special laser beam aimed at a target made of rare, manmade compound in an experiment within FSU's Center for Materials Research and Technology. Photo by Ray Stanyard, FSU Office of Research.

high-temperature superconductivity and in microelectronics. Collaborating with the University of Florida's materials science program, Microfabritech, MARTECH researchers specialize in using beams of ions and atoms to develop and test materials with new and unusual electrical, magnetic, and optical properties.

• The Learning Systems Institute (LSI)—Since 1984 this world-renowned educational research program has attracted more than $100 million in federal grants, enabling it to become the nation's chief exporter of what is known as ISD (instructional systems design)-based training technology to third world countries in Africa, Asia, and the Caribbean. LSI's central mission is the application of ISD technology to solve large-scale training and education problems both in schools and industry.

FROM LAB TO MARKET

The prodigious talents exhibited by these and other FSU research components are finding increasing application in industry, thanks to Florida State's stepped-up emphasis on technology transfer. In recent years, efforts to find ways to move FSU lab discoveries into the marketplace have produced substantial returns for both the university and campus researchers.

So far, the best example of FSU technology transfer is a licensing agreement the university holds with a major pharmaceutical company, Bristol-Myers Squibb. The company has an exclusive right to use a patent the university holds on the synthesis of the drug taxol, which is one of the most important

The business end of FSU's Tandem Van de Graaff nuclear accelerator is this 60-foot-long linear accelerator complex. Capabilities of FSU's Nuclear Research Program rival those of some of the largest nuclear accelerator programs in the nation. Photo by Ray Stanyard, FSU Office of Research.

anticancer agents to emerge in the past decade. During fiscal year '93-'94, Florida State received nearly $6 million in licensing revenues derived from the taxol patent, which is based on work conducted by a university organic chemist who is considered the world's leading authority in taxol chemistry.

RESEARCH AT YOUR SERVICE

No public university takes its responsibility for public service more seriously than does Florida State. Helping Florida's various governments solve sticky problems, in fact, has become an FSU specialty over the years.

Much of the campus's public outreach is conducted through an administrative arm based at Innovation Park. Founded in 1973, the Institute of Science and Public Affairs (ISPA) serves as an umbrella organization for 17 research and public service centers all based at FSU. The institute provides these centers with administrative support and helps coordinate their objectives with those of the Florida Legislature and state, local, and regional agencies.

ISPA-associated centers help public policy makers throughout the state wrestle with dilemmas ranging from handling hazardous wastes to providing better care for the state's large elderly population. Such help is welcomed by Florida governments having to deal with a population that since the mid-1980s has been growing at the rate of 900 newcomers a day.

Vice President Al Gore was present for the October 1, 1994 dedication of the National High Magnetic Field Laboratory, headquartered on FSU's campus. Photo by Ray Stanyard, FSU Office of Research.

AN ARTFUL TRADITION

Florida State University's successful forays into the realms of science and technology are surely remarkable for what they say about its innovative and aggressive scientists, engineers, and technicians. However, such success may have taken its cue from a much older FSU tradition that in many quarters is still regarded as among the best American academe has to offer.

Nurtured by roots firmly entrenched in its historic liberal arts calling, Florida State is a renowned center for graduate education and training in the visual and performing arts. The university's schools of dance, music, and theater are generally regarded as the finest in the Southeast, with strong national followings based in California, New York, and elsewhere where there's a high demand for exemplary talent in the performing arts.

In 1989 the Florida Legislature established the FSU Conservatory of Motion Picture, Television, and Recording Arts, creating the state's only film school—one of only seven in the nation. With its graduate (MFA) program based at the Asolo Performing Arts Center in Sarasota, Florida, the school has galvanized the attention of the state's promising film industry by producing an extraordinarily talented pool of filmmakers and film specialists whose credentials are rapidly gaining a worldwide reputation.

TOWARD THE NEXT 50

As Florida State approaches its mid-century mark, the university's future has never appeared brighter. During the past half-century, a rich tradition in the arts and humanities has coalesced with a newer mission in research to produce a clear message: Florida State University is truly one of the South's most lucrative settings for higher learning in almost any field you can name. A tradition in excellence is only getting better with age. ◆

TALLAHASSEE
MEMORIAL REGIONAL
MEDICAL CENTER

From the beginning, setting a high standard of excellence without losing sight of the human element of medicine has been the hallmark of Tallahassee Memorial Regional Medical Center. As it has grown to be one of the largest medical centers in the Southeast and truly regional in its service area, Tallahassee Memorial has kept its close ties to the community that first saw the need for a high quality hospital facility 45 years ago.

At the end of World War II, Tallahassee's medical facilities consisted of several small medical clinics, some dating from the Civil War. The only hospital was located at Dale Mabry Field (the old airport, used by the military during World War II) and was due to be shut down soon after the war. Through the work of community volunteers, a new building was built and occupied at its present site in 1948. Volunteerism remains an integral part of the Medical Center. To this day Tallahassee Memorial is governed by a volunteer, community board of directors.

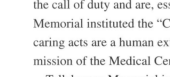

The extraordinary volunteer founding and design of the original facility are reflected today in Tallahassee Memorial's "Caring Hands" approach to its patients and their families. Tallahassee Memorial serves patients from a 120-mile radius with a philosophy which says "our hands are different." The care and concern with which everyone serves results in hundreds of daily acts of kindness and compassion. It is Tallahassee Memorial's belief that, when noticed and rewarded, compassionate acts spawn other, similar acts. To recognize employees' special efforts that go above and beyond the call of duty and are, essentially, voluntary, Tallahassee Memorial instituted the "Caring Hands" award program. These caring acts are a human extension of the medical and technical mission of the Medical Center.

Tallahassee Memorial is a full service, acute care facility. It maintains the oldest cancer treatment program in Florida continually certified by the American College of Surgeons. Also, there are many specialty care units, called Centers of

Tallahassee Memorial Regional Medical Center is the seventh largest hospital in Florida, offering state-of-the-art wellness, diagnostic, and treatment services to residents in a 16-county region surrounding Tallahassee.

Excellence, where the specific needs of Tallahassee Memorial patients are addressed. The Heart Institute, the Diabetes Center, the Psychiatric Center, the Women's Pavilion, and the NeuroScience Center all provide prevention and educational services as well as clinical care. These services speak directly to the Medical Center board of directors' determination to make Tallahassee Memorial a premier medical facility.

Within Tallahassee Memorial's seven-story structure are five specialized intensive care units (ICUs). Every day the physicians and staff of the Pediatric, Neurology, Cardiac, Medical/Surgical, and Cardiovascular/Surgical ICUs vigorously attend to the most critically ill patients. Each unit's specialization allows staff to hone the skills necessary to meet their patients' care needs. Perhaps no unit in the Medical Center is as heart-wrenching as the Newborn Intensive Care Unit, where tiny babies fight for their lives under the watchful eyes of specially trained neonatologists and pediatric staff. The only high-risk nursery serving the region, this unit cares for premature, critically-ill infants with the latest in technology, the most human of hearts, and an eye toward innovation. Tallahassee Memorial's Newborn Intensive Care Unit was one

The Newborn Intensive Care Unit's specially trained nurses and staff care for babies as small as one pound, and other newborns experiencing medical complications.

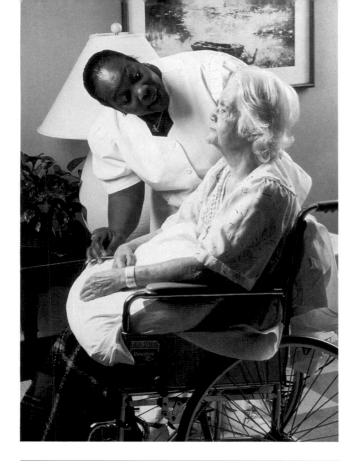

Tallahassee Memorial's Long Term Care Facility offers personalized, compassionate care for those needing skilled nursing care in a home-like atmosphere.

of the first in the country to practice "kangaroo care." This method, discovered by researchers in South America, places the naked premature infant on the bare chest of its mother or father. Research has shown that this reduces the infant's stress level and improves the rate of recovery. Tallahassee Memorial was also one of the test sites for a drug that helps premature infants' underdeveloped lungs better capture the oxygen they need to survive.

Like many hospitals today, Tallahassee Memorial dedicates a great deal of effort and resources to education and prevention as ways to reduce illness and injury, to improve patients' overall well-being and recovery rates, and to reduce health care costs. The Heart Institute at Tallahassee Memorial conducts research on heart disease and its treatments while focusing on public and professional education. In addition, it operates the Heart Network, which provides consulting and educational services to rural hospitals within the Medical Center's service area. Tallahassee Memorial is the region's major provider of open-heart surgery services since the first procedure was performed at the Medical Center in 1974. Cardiovascular surgeons also performed the area's first heart transplant in 1985. A complete range of diagnostic and treatment programs related to cardiac care is offered at the Medical Center, including heart catheterization, cardiovascular lab, and cardiac rehabilitation. The Heart Institute offers a substantial public education calendar, including cardiac patient support groups, weight reduction programs that follow heart-healthy diets, Smoke Stoppers to aid in quitting smoking, basic heart information courses, walking and fitness classes, chest pain alert

campaigns, and more. Proving that it is never too early to start living healthy, the Heart Institute coordinates a Healthy Hearts for Children program in public schools which provides innovative and interactive programming on healthy lifestyles to first, second, and third-graders.

An important adjunct service of the Heart Institute is the Corporate Wellness program, a series of services designed to keep employees healthy and productive at work. The program aims to eliminate poor lifestyle choices and bad habits through education and participation in activities such as weight loss, smoking cessation, increased exercise, quick recognition of trouble signs, and even lifesaving technique training.

Another Center of Excellence is the NeuroScience Center. This center combines the best in assessment and treatment of neurological and neuromuscular afflictions through a highly trained, qualified, and multidisciplinary staff of neurologists, neurology-certified nurses, patient educators, social workers, and physical, occupational, and speech therapists. These specialists are supported by the medical staff and critical care facilities of Tallahassee Memorial, including the Department of Neurological Surgery and Neurodiagnostics. The goal of the center is to serve the medical and general community with innovation in neurological treatment and education, and to serve as a resource and referral base for treatment of neuromuscular disorders, including headaches, head injury, sleep disorders, Parkinson's disease, balance problems, and other neurological conditions and injuries. The center coordinates support groups for brain injury, headache, and Parkinson's disease in association with other community organizations.

Tallahassee Memorial is one of only nine hospitals in Florida with designation by the state as an acute spinal cord injury center, the only such center between Jacksonville and Pensacola. Prevention of spinal cord injuries is an important part of this designation. With this in mind, the NeuroScience Center conducts a regular series of physician conferences and community-wide events to promote head and spinal cord injury prevention.

The Atrium, a striking new entranceway for patients, visitors, and their families, provides a central information point and easy access to a variety of services at the Medical Center and the two professional office buildings located on campus.

The Psychiatric Center is another specialty unit at Tallahassee Memorial. It offers programs to help people deal with and overcome depression and mental illnesses in three specialty areas: geriatrics, adolescence, and general psychiatric

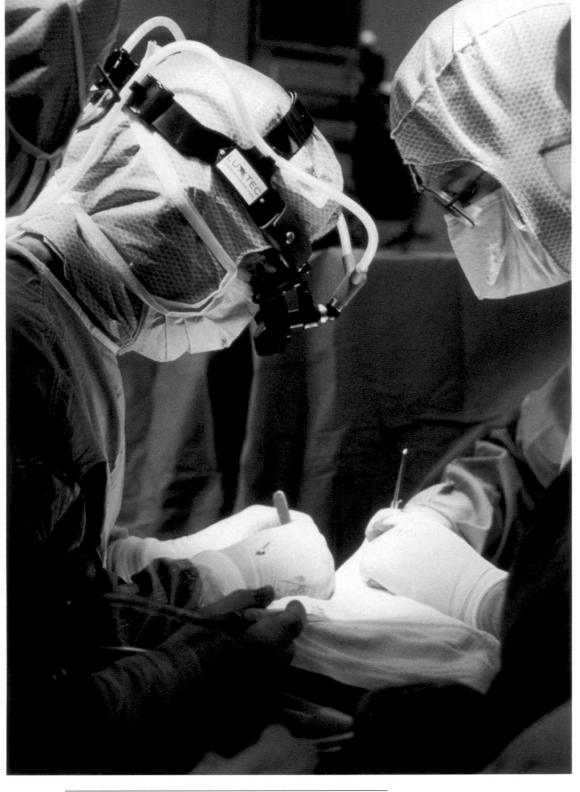

Tallahassee Memorial's heart surgery program is supported by experienced, highly skilled physicians, nurses, and staff. Heart surgery is one component of a comprehensive cardiovascular program at the Medical Center which includes education, screenings, prevention, diagnostic, and treatment services.

Programs are residential and outpatient in this free-standing facility located next to the Medical Center. Its location simultaneously provides convenient access and privacy.

The Diabetes Center at Tallahassee Memorial was created to provide physician support to treat diabetes mellitus, a complex endocrine disorder. Its major role is to offer education and training to assist physicians in assessing the numerous variables which impact sugar control. The Diabetes Center boasts one of the few psychologists in the nation with dual certification as a diabetes educator. This innovation is just one of the qualities that make the center, affiliated with the International Diabetes Center in Minneapolis, an excellent resource for people in the Southeast with diabetes. The Diabetes Center staff encourage their patients to work as part of a team of specialists—endocrinologists, certified diabetes educator nurses, dieticians, exercise specialists, and counselors—in the management of their disease. The center publishes *The Glucose Gazette* to keep patients abreast of the latest in technology and local activities, to pass along manufacturers' savings, and to encourage participation in support groups. Group courses, individual counseling, medical care, support meetings, and beginning exercise classes are all part of staying actively healthy, which is the goal for every Diabetes Center patient.

illness. The adolescents' and children's program provide treatment for children and adolescents who are experiencing episodes of adjustment disorders, conduct disorders, depression, or major mental illness such as schizophrenia. Senior adult patients experiencing psychiatric symptoms of confusion, disorientation, delusions or hallucinations, and major depressions are provided care and treatment through the Senior Adult Services program. The Adult Specialty Care Unit is self-contained to afford the patient with an environment which promotes reality-based interactions and experiences.

Another program that aims to include the consumer in all major decisions and, indeed, to improve each participant's control over her life, is the Women's Pavilion. The pavilion houses the Women's Resource Center, the Mammography Suite, the Birth Place, and the Family Care Unit. Meeting the demand for female patient education, the Women's Resource Center rapidly became and remains the region's premier resource for

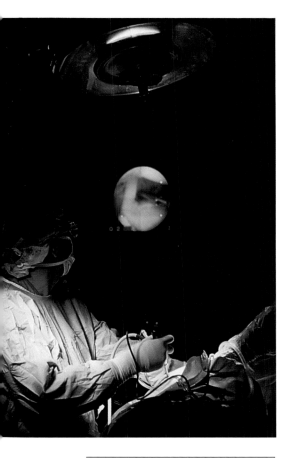

Through the use of state-of-the-art technology, like laparoscopy, surgeons are able to reduce a patient's recovery time. This technology allows the surgeon to perform surgery inside the body without creating large incisions. Video images taken inside the body are displayed on a television screen while the surgeon is operating.

female physical, emotional, and mental health needs. The Woman-to-Woman program educates women facing breast surgery, and the Breast Prosthesis Service is available for women who choose to wear a prosthesis following breast surgery. All services are augmented by support groups, and a resource library is open to women everywhere who seek to learn more about their bodies, their health or illness, and their lives. Just as in the other specialty units, the Women's Pavilion is heavily invested in outreach and education, providing a full calendar of workshops, seminars, and a "Brunch 'n Learn" series throughout the year. These resources and events provide citizens throughout the region with the most up-to-date information available on a variety of issues and topics, from infant/child CPR to advances in infertility, from coping with chronic pain to dealing effectively with life's problems.

In an emergency, Tallahassee Memorial's ambulance and LifeFlight services provide 24-hour emergency medical care. LifeFlight, the air ambulance service inaugurated by Tallahassee Memorial in 1981, has expanded the hospital's transportation service to a 90-mile radius. Since its inception, LifeFlight has saved hundreds of lives, and its paramedics and nurses have won numerous awards, including top emergency-services helicopter pilot in the United States. No award is so touching, perhaps, as the cards and letters from grateful patients and family members who realize the difference that precious transport time has made in their lives.

In Leon County, Tallahassee Memorial is the sole provider of emergency ambulance services. The endeavor is a huge commitment of manpower and resources. The Medical Center has provided ambulances without local tax support since 1972. The service exceeds state requirements by providing Advanced Life Support services, with most ambulance crews comprised of two certified paramedics who are Advanced Life Support certified. Staffed by over 80 registered nurses, paramedics, and emergency medical technician dispatchers, the EMS has improved response time to emergencies through the use of the Computer Aided Dispatch System and an enhanced 911 emergency telephone system.

Tallahassee Memorial is blessed with tremendous public support of its medical goals through fund-raising. With almost 800 licensed beds and serving more than 200,000 patients each year, the resource demands at Tallahassee Memorial Regional Medical Center never cease. One of the premier events in Tallahassee each year is the Golden Gala. Begun in 1984, each gala has seen national and international stars perform for appreciative audiences who routinely raise tens of thousands of dollars for equipment, services, and technology. From Barbara Mandrell to Wayne Newton, the stars have come out to sing the praises of and ensure that quality medical care is available to the community through Tallahassee Memorial Regional Medical Center. Funds raised through the Golden Gala allow the Medical Center to provide the latest in high technology, enhance clinical care, and ensure future health care staff needs through gift scholarships.

With its Centers of Excellence, its Caring Hands approach, and its business efficiency, Tallahassee Memorial has been on the cutting edge of the rapidly changing health care market for many years. The board of directors looks to the future of health care in the region and sees Tallahassee Memorial playing a dominant role in assuring the finest quality of care for the region. ◆

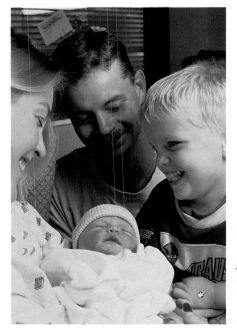

The Family Care Unit encourages families to enjoy their special moments together in a nurturing environment.

From the warm, inviting lobby to the sophisticated volunteer program, everything about Tallahassee Community Hospital is geared toward making each patient and family member's experience as comfortable as possible. As a subsidiary of Columbia/HCA Healthcare Corporation, the largest health care corporation in the world, Community Hospital operates on a distinctly human scale.

TALLAHASSEE COMMUNITY HOSPITAL

cardiac surgeons in the region, is actually a full continuum of care from education and prevention to recovery and rehabilitation. The hospital's annual event, HeartWatch, provides a complete screening for cardiac health as a community service to local residents.

Another annual event, the Baby Fair, introduces prospective and new parents to the expected and unexpected aspects of pregnancy, birth, and parenting. Tours of the Family Center, a special wing with its own entrance, demonstrate the comfortable birth suites. The Family Center provides comprehensive, family-centered maternity care based on the idea that a new mother is delivered with each new baby. For siblings, there are special classes and tours for the equally expectant big brothers and sisters of the newborn. A unique aspect to each new mother's stay at the Family Center is "Shared Care," a nursing concept that assigns one nurse to mother and child.

Begun in 1979, Community Hospital is a full-service acute care facility whose surgical suite is equipped with the latest technology to support physicians in a number of surgical specialties. These include cardiovascular (open heart) and peripheral vascular surgery, gynecology, neurosurgery, opthamology, orthopedic surgery, otolaryngology, plastic surgery, urology, and general surgery, as well as laser surgery. The hospital's Critical Care Department includes an Intensive Care Unit and a Progressive Care Unit that treat surgical and medical patients. The Cardiac Surgery Intensive Care Unit is reserved for heart/thoracic surgery patients. In addition, a separate Ambulatory Services Department for single-day procedures provides Tallahasseans and physicians with a wide variety of surgical and outpatient options. To speed the healing process whenever necessary, Community Hospital operates one of the few Multiplace Hyperbaric Chambers in the region.

Columbia/HCA Tallahassee Community Hospital has been in service to the residents of the Big Bend area of Florida since 1979. A fully-accredited, acute care facility, Community Hospital has 180 state-licensed beds and has a well-earned reputation for combining skill, technology, and personal attention in a quality patient care setting.

The hospital has earned a reputation for personal care and attention, due in part to its innovative Nurse Case Management Program. Implemented in 1989, this patient-centered delivery system provides a collaborative team approach to managing patients' health care before, during, and after their hospital stay. Each case manager is a bachelor-degreed registered nurse, clinically-oriented, with advanced training in resource management and performance improvement. In addition to coordinating the care for a set of doctors' patients and working directly with the patient and family, the case managers review practice patterns from pre-op to discharge and aftercare.

Other programs take a comprehensive, coordinated approach to patient care and well-being, too. For example, the Cardiac Program, supported by the finest cardiologists and

The notion that Tallahassee Community Hospital serves patients and family members who are customers and guests spawned the Guest Relations Program, an approach perhaps more familiar to the hospitality industry than to the health care system. Trained volunteers visit patients the day after admission and twice weekly thereafter. Information about the program is at each patient's bedside, including a phone number for instant contact with Guest Relations personnel for immediate help in resolving concerns or answering questions. A Patient Information Booklet advises family and friends on all hospital procedures from admission to discharge. In this age of high technology, the purpose of the Guest Relations Program is to provide a personal touch with patients.

Perhaps because its mission statement was developed by the employees through a series of meetings and is frequently reviewed and updated, it is in practice every day at Community Hospital: "We believe in a personal commitment to providing

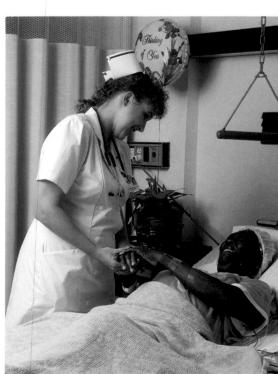

Patients at Tallahassee Community Hospital receive quality, compassionate care. Community Hospital employs more than 250 highly-skilled professional nurses such as cardiovascular, intensive care, surgical, or medical/surgical.

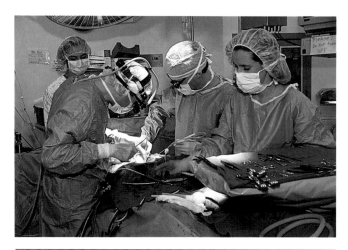

Tallahassee Community Hospital's surgical services include a comprehensive open heart surgery program, orthopedic, gynecological, and general surgeries.

professional and compassionate health care. At Community Hospital, achieving quality means the continuous improvement of services to meet the needs and expectations of the patients, the physicians, the employees, and the communities we serve." Similarly, Community Hospital's vision statement is a way of providing care, doing business, and being known throughout the region, not just a dusty set of words filed away somewhere: "At Community Hospital, we are community-centered, results-oriented, and continuously improving. We will be known as a hospital which is most sensitive to the individual needs of our patients, physicians, and employees, with a reputation for quality, family-centered care, earning complete community confidence in each of our service areas."

To encourage these attitudes in future employees and to help serve Tallahassee's education needs, Community Hospital participates extensively in the Blueprint program in conjunction with the Leon County Schools Division of Vocational, Adult, and Community Education. Blueprint is a career exploration experience for area eighth graders interested in health care. In five years of participation, more than 2,500 students have shadowed hospital staff in 15 departments. In 1994 Tallahassee Community Hospital won recognition for its involvement with Blueprint by winning the prestigious statewide Business Recognition Award from the Florida Department of Education and the Tallahassee Business Volunteer of the Year Award.

Outreach from Community Hospital is just as important as in-facility services. The recent acquisition of nearby walk-in physician clinics provides patients with a coordinated health care delivery system. And, because Tallahassee serves as a regional focal point for all kinds of health care services, Community Hospital provides primary and specialty care in surrounding counties. On a regular schedule, hospital-affiliated physicians travel to neighboring counties to consult with patients and other physicians, prepare patients for in-hospital procedures, and often prevent unnecessary hospital stays in these specialty care clinics.

To further the outreach effort, Community Hospital provides a Physician Referral Line, free to all callers, and provides Business Health Services to area employers. In addition to well-known programs such as Drug-free Workplace, BHS helps employers keep their workforces healthy through prevention and education programs, workers compensation treatment and follow-up, the Communicare Center, a well-equipped rehabilitation and physical therapy facility operates a fitness center that is open to the public, and provides a specially trained staff of experts to assist patients in rehabilitative recovery. Again in the outreach mode, the "Walk About" program offers fitness walking for area residents in conjunction with the Tallahassee Mall.

Several other specialty services keep Community Hospital at the forefront, meeting citizens' needs in Tallahassee. The Addiction Recovery Center offers residential and inpatient services to individuals with drug and alcohol addictions. The Diagnostic Sleep Center evaluates a full range of sleep disorders. And a Speakers Bureau of nurses, physicians, social workers, and administrators rounds out the hospital's community outreach efforts. This free service allows Community Hospital to share important health information with Tallahassee and surrounding areas.

The economic impact of Community Hospital is just as profound as the health care offerings. More than 700 people are employed, and the hospital is the sixth largest taxpayer in Leon County. The future is bright for Tallahassee Community Hospital. By adhering to a community-oriented philosophy and a patient and family-centered method of dispensing health care, Community Hospital is sure to continue as an integral part of the community—just as the name says. ◆

Community Hospital's annual Baby Fair brings more than 2,000 residents to the hospital each year. Participants enjoy a variety of events, from a lecture series by obstetricians and allied health professionals to entertainment for all ages. In 1994, the hospital's Family Center celebrated 10 years of service to the community.

E very student is a promise with great potential at North Florida Christian School. The school's mission is to provide students with a quality, Christian education. At NFCS, we teach the fundamental skills that enable students to earn a living and life skills with Christian values to teach students how to live.

Started in 1966, the school is one of the ministries of Temple Baptist Church. Other ministries of Temple are The Lighthouse Children's Home, Haven of Rest Rescue Mission, and Television Station W65BG. Many of the school's 1,500 students and their families are members of Temple Baptist, and others represent a variety of denominations. At NFCS, students and parents find excellence in

NORTH FLORIDA CHRISTIAN SCHOOL

"The Christian education of our children is a vital task that requires unwavering commitment in the face of increasing pressures and attacks on our youth today. I personally believe that we can realize our greatest success when we work together in the home, the church, and in the Christian school."

NFCS is accredited by the Florida Association of Christian Schools. Each faculty member and support staff acknowledges a personal commitment to Christ and believes that the work of the classroom is the work of the Lord. Teachers have college degrees and are certified by the FACCS. The school promotes and rewards continuing education by its faculty.

NFCS has a reputation for academic excellence, with achievement scores that are higher than average. Success in interscholastic athletic competition is also a point of excellence at NFCS. The NFCS Eagles are perennial contenders in FHSAA district and regional football and baseball. The girls' fast pitch softball team has ranked second in the state, and there is FHSAA basketball for girls and boys. Annual science fairs always have NFCS representatives winning top honors in local, state, and international events.

There are classes from pre-kindergarten through high school on a 30-acre campus that features an outstanding football facility, track, newly refurbished gymnasium, and classrooms. Targeting a modest student/teacher ratio allows for individual attention in each child's day. For students who learn better working at their own pace, the school offers Accelerated Christian Education classes. There are aftercare programs for younger students and numerous extracurricular offerings for older students, including art, drama, and music. Summer programs are available, and several transportation options make the school accessible to students in neighboring counties.

The wide variety of elective classes includes physics, chemistry, biology, Latin, psychology, and various computer courses. Students graduating from North Florida Christian School are prepared. Whether plans call for working, attending vocational school, or seeking higher education, as most do, NFCS graduates are ready.

By challenging a student's mind, promoting physical exercise, encouraging extracurricular activity, and training for the Christian life, North Florida Christian School prepares students to live successfully. Deeply rooted, with an eye toward the future, NFCS promotes values that last a lifetime. ◆

A fully equipped laboratory is available to students of North Florida Christian to pursue courses in all areas of scientific studies.

Elementary students take advantage of a wide range of reading materials in the elementary library. A second library for high school students offers a variety of fiction, nonfiction, and reference materials.

education, outstanding athletic programs, and many services and extracurricular activities rarely found in private schools. The program is academic, athletic, social, and uniquely Christian. Says Dr. Randy Ray, pastor of Temple Baptist and president of North Florida Christian School:

Quality health care in the Tallahassee area is assured for members of the city's first and largest health maintenance organization, Capital Health Plan. CHP's mission, defined at the outset and highly appropriate in the changing climate of health care reform, is "to meet the needs of the residents of North Florida for comprehensive and high quality health care services in a cost-effective and efficient manner."

CAPITAL
HEALTH PLAN

Begun in 1982 by a group of local citizens concerned with the rising cost of health care and the need for an alternative system of health care delivery, Capital Health Plan has been an industry leader and on the cutting edge of HMO development from the start. It was the first area HMO to receive one year accreditation from the National Committee on Quality Assurance and the only area HMO to be federally qualified. Unusual in its nonprofit status, the plan operates not to provide a return on investment, but to serve the community. Revenues stay in the community and are plowed back into expanded services, used to improve benefits and facilities, and to keep rates down.

One in five people in Tallahassee and the surrounding counties are members of Capital Health Plan. The plan operates as a mixed model HMO, combining the advantages of affiliated primary care physicians and of a centralized health center complex that provides members with "one-stop shopping." Hundreds of area physicians have been affiliated with CHP for many years. The complex on Centerville Road boasts private office modules for physicians, a laboratory, an eye care center, x-ray, and a pharmacy. Members can park once and easily walk to all of these services. Other members prefer the traditional office setting of a smaller physician practice and these are also available under the plan.

This choice of access is an outward representation of the plan's basic mission of providing broadly accessible health care. CHP emphasizes preventive care and wellness, but keeps

special late hours to accommodate medical emergencies. Should someone need a health service not locally available, Capital Health Plan has partnered with the Mayo Clinic in Jacksonville, Florida, and the University of Florida Medical School in Gainesville. These tertiary relationships back up an excellent local medical community and give members wide access to very sophisticated health care.

Access to affordable, quality health care is not a problem for small employers in Tallahassee, because CHP has made coverage for these businesses and individuals a priority. More than 800 small businesses are members of the plan, which minimizes cost sharing, thus providing these firms with reliable budget figures and access to quality health care.

Physicians are attracted to Capital Health Plan because the environment is optimal for taking care of patients. Because coverage is so comprehensive, they have less concern about whether patients will take advantage of recommended treatments.

Capital Health Plan's mission is "to meet the needs of the residents of North Florida for comprehensive and high quality health care services in a cost-effective and efficient manner."

CHP carries on its mission of providing access to high quality health care in its corporate citizenship activities. The plan sees itself as a catalyst, taking the initiative in promoting and supporting health care in the local community. To this end, the medical staff participates in a variety of community service activities including volunteering at local public health clinics and providing free physical examinations for female high school athletes in the area. The plan and its staff are also involved in supporting many health-related community efforts from promoting breast cancer awareness with the American Cancer Society to actively participating in the annual March of Dimes Walk-A-Thon.

While the future of health care reform is uncertain, Capital Health Plan's is secure. As a leader forging the new landscape of affordable, quality health care services, CHP has created the very environment that makes it possible for individuals and businesses to get the health care they need at a price they can afford with a benefit package that attracts and keeps good employees. ◆

Unusual in its nonprofit status, CHP operates not for return on investment, but to serve the community. Revenues stay in the community and are plowed back into expanded services, used to improve the benefits and facilities, and to keep rates down.

In 1973 two young orthopedic surgery residents at Emory University Hospital shared a dream of creating a sports medicine center in Tallahassee, Florida. Dr. Doug Henderson opened his practice later that year, and he was joined in 1975 by Dr. Tom Haney. Together, they pioneered arthroscopic surgery and sports medicine in north Florida. From this nucleus, their dream gradually became the reality of the Tallahassee Orthopedic Clinic, one of the largest and best known orthopedic practices in the South.

Today TOC consists of 12 physicians who subspecialize in all aspects of orthopedic care. The physicians are best known as the team physicians for Florida State University, Florida A & M University, Tallahassee Community College, and approximately 50 high schools. However, they also regularly care for the elderly, the nonathlete, and children and all their orthopedic needs. The subspecialty interest areas include arthroscopy, joint replacement, hand, spine, foot, and pediatric orthopedics, and sports medicine.

The clinic includes 10 orthopedic surgeons: Drs. Haney, Henderson, Schmidt, Thornberry, Wingo, Dewey, Lyon, Jordan, Fahey, and Berg. Two family practice physicians, Drs. Stowers and Alexander, provide conservative and diagnostic musculoskeletal care. TOC physicians are located in the Tallahassee Orthopedic Center, a 60,000-square-foot state-of-the-art medical mall, and in the Professional Office Building of Tallahassee Memorial Regional Medical Center.

The goal of TOC is to provide expedient and concerned care for their patients. Every attempt is made to evaluate and treat injuries as soon as possible. They follow a conservative philosophy that saves surgery as the last

TALLAHASSEE ORTHOPEDIC CLINIC

resort in attempts to get patients back to work or play as soon as feasible.

Tallahassee has become a center for sports activities in the region. This includes the nationally recognized sports program at FSU, FAMU, and TCC, a professional hockey team, the training site for the British Olympians, active city league and intramural sports, as well as high school sports. Tallahassee has also hosted the Special Olympics, the Sunshine State Games, and the Law Enforcement Games. For these events the Tallahassee Orthopedic Clinic has been called on to provide orthopedic care for competing athletes. The same philosophy of quality care and rapid recovery is applied not only to the athletic population, but also to all patients seen at the Tallahassee Orthopedic Clinic.

The physicians of TOC have been instrumental in developing and providing trainers for Tallahassee area high schools. Every Friday night during football season, a medical team from the Tallahassee Orthopedic Clinic/Tallahassee Sports Medicine provides coverage for several high school football teams within a 75-mile radius of Tallahassee. Prior to the season, TOC physicians give free seminars to area high school coaches and trainers covering injury prevention, heat illness, injury recognition, and the care of injured athletes on the field. Tallahassee Orthopedic Clinic/Tallahassee Sports Medicine has helped to provide trainers who are on staff a half day at each Tallahassee high school during practice to prevent potential injuries and to give the athletes the best possible immediate attention when accidents occur.

Tallahassee Orthopedic Clinic physicians are actively involved in the community. The clinic is a charter corporate sponsor of the Tallahassee Area Sports Hall of Fame. Each year, TOC sponsors the Winter Festival with its ice skating rink gracing one of the nation's southernmost capitals. TOC also helps sponsor such events as the annual March of Dimes Walk-A-Thon, the American Heart Association Walk-A-Thon, tennis tournaments, and various road races. TOC physicians are active in supporting the elderly members of the community. Physicians give presentations to residents in area residential communities for the elderly covering such subjects as avoiding hip fractures and stretching and fitness programs.

As Tallahassee grows, so does the Tallahassee Orthopedic Clinic. Caring for approximately 75,000 patients each year, TOC is a true reflection of the growth of Tallahassee and its interest in sports and fitness. ◆

Tallahassee Orthopedic Clinic physicians are actively involved in the community. Shown here, Dr. Tom Haney and number 35, Sean Jackson, help 1993 Heisman Trophy winner, Charlie Ward, off the field during the 1993 FSU/Wake Forest game.

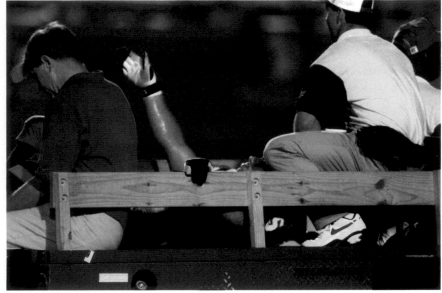

The goal of TOC is to provide expedient and concerned care for their patients. Every attempt is made to evaluate and treat injuries as soon as possible. Pictured, Dr. Doug Henderson assists injured Enzo Laureano. Despite his injury, Laureano still supports his team with the famous "Nole Chop."

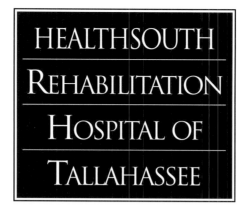

HEALTHSOUTH REHABILITATION HOSPITAL OF TALLAHASSEE

"Getting people back . . . to work . . . to play . . . to living" is the goal of every employee at HEALTHSOUTH Tallahassee. The full-service, 70-bed rehabilitation hospital "bridges the gap" between a patient's traumatic injury, disabling illness, or crippling disease to an independent and productive lifestyle. The hospital is the only one of its kind in the region, and is a part of the HEALTHSOUTH Corporation, the largest provider of comprehensive rehabilitation services in the country.

Tallahassee's HEALTHSOUTH Rehabilitation team provides a full continuum of services from inpatient to day treatment to outpatient therapy for children and adults with a brain injury, spinal cord injury, stroke, orthopedic injury, and many other disabling illnesses. The hospital is accredited by the Joint Commission on the Accreditation of Healthcare Organizations and the Commission on Accreditation of Rehabilitation Facilities.

The hospital's team of more than 100 specialists work together to provide patients with the highest quality outcome at the most efficient cost. A physiatrist, a medical doctor board certified in physical medicine and rehabilitation, leads the rehabilitation team and oversees each patient's care. Rehabilitation includes the physical as well as the emotional aspects of recovery through patient and family education and extensive therapies. As a part of the rehabilitation process, occupational, physical, speech, and respiratory therapists work side by side with physicians, rehabilitation nurses, therapeutic recreation specialists, neuropsychologists, dieticians, vocational rehabilitation specialists and case managers.

Each member of the rehabilitation team is personally involved in the patient's recovery, rejoicing over accomplishments and working with the patient's family to overcome any setbacks.

Furthermore, the team provides training for the family to help them adjust to the patient's new circumstances. Assistance is provided in such areas as home modifications, equipment, and community resources.

At HEALTHSOUTH Rehabilitation Hospital of Tallahassee, the comprehensive team approach to rehabilitation ensures that the needs of the patient, the family, employers, insurers, physicians, and the community are met throughout the challenging process of recovery.

As more people survive traumatic events such as automobile and work-related accidents, and as the population ages, the demand for rehabilitation services continues to increase. We are prepared to meet this demand with the most comprehensive rehabilitation services in the region.

HEALTHSOUTH is proud to be a part of Tallahassee. Care for our community is shown every day by getting people back—to work, to play, to living. ◆

Each member of the rehabilitation team is personally involved in the patient's recovery, rejoicing over accomplishments and working with the patient's family to overcome any setbacks.

HEALTHSOUTH Tallahassee, a full-service, 70-bed rehabilitation hospital "bridges the gap" between a patient's traumatic injury, disabling illness, or crippling disease to an independent and productive lifestyle.

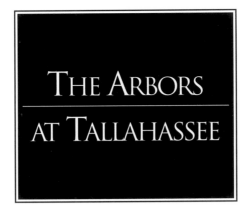

THE ARBORS
AT TALLAHASSEE

In an era of health care reform and a universal need to minimize health care costs, the Arbors at Tallahassee is delivering high quality, professional services that people can afford in a pleasant, home-away-from-home atmosphere.

The Arbors is a 120-bed facility that provides two essential services—general and restorative (long-term) care for patients who can no longer live at home, and subacute care for patients who are ready to leave a hospital setting but need rehabilitative or complex medical services before returning home.

The 60-bed general and restorative care unit provides traditional skilled nursing facility care and services. Patients live in semiprivate rooms decorated with residential quality furniture and their own belongings. A private dining room and living room allow families to gather intimately for their own unique celebrations of birthdays, anniversaries, and holidays. A busy recreational calendar and spacious television and activity rooms provide plenty of diversion and enjoyment. The dining room offerings are restaurant quality, and the decor is elegant, with cloth, glass, and silverware accoutrements.

What makes the Arbors unique, however, is its 60-bed specialized subacute care unit. The subacute care approach

to rehabilitation and recovery was developed by the Arbors' parent firm, Arbor Health Care Company. The concept came about in response to two main factors—hospitals' economic incentives to discharge Medicare patients sooner, and managed care companies' need to find low-cost alternatives to hospital care. By using a skilled nursing center to deliver services, the Arbor subacute care concept delivers services at 30 to 60 percent of the cost of acute hospital care. The Arbors at Tallahassee is certified by the State of Florida as a skilled nursing facility and has received a superior rating from the Joint Commission on Accreditation of Healthcare Organizations.

Patients who benefit from staying at the Arbors at Tallahassee typically need three to eight hours of nursing care per day. A physician-directed, interdisciplinary team approach is used to meet the comprehensive needs of each patient. These teams establish goals for the patients, monitor their progress, modify the treatment plan when necessary, and integrate the patients' nursing care with their therapy regimen.

Subacute care at the Arbors is provided around four major programs—medical rehabilitation, respiratory care, infusion therapy, and wound care. Approximately 24 therapists are on staff, and the nurse-to-patient ratio is about one to eight. Discharge planning begins the day a person arrives at the Arbors to ensure the smoothest possible transition from the facility to home or other placement.

Much of the rehabilitation that occurs at the Arbors involves occupational therapy for the adjustment to daily living chores such as cooking and cleaning that make recovery successful. To meet this important need, the Arbors has expanded its physical therapy department with the addition of 900 square feet of space that includes a fully functional kitchen. Some 98 percent of the Arbors' patients receive physical therapy and are in aggressive rehabilitation programs. Other rehabilitation therapies include speech, physical, and respiratory areas.

The demand for the Arbors has exceeded Arbor Health Care Company's expectations, as physicians, discharge planners, and case managers from hospitals and other referral sources have embraced the subacute care concept. The Arbors at Tallahassee is the only such facility between Jacksonville, Pensacola, and Gainesville, and serves several counties in south Georgia as well.

Recovery from major illness or surgery is difficult, and the decision to stay in or place a loved one in long-term care is stressful, at best. The Arbors at Tallahassee provides a high quality, professional, and affordable response to these health care needs. ◆

The Arbors at Tallahassee provides a high quality, professional, and affordable response to recovery from major illness or surgery.

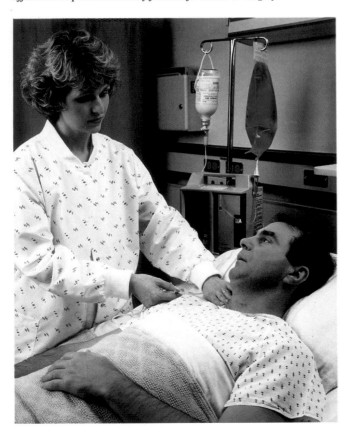

The most frequent comment patients make about their experience with Tallahassee Single Day Surgery Center is how personally they feel they were treated. This distinction reflects the center's motto, "our caring staff singles us out." Started in 1978 as an alternative to overnight hospital stays for procedures that could be performed on an outpatient basis, Tallahassee Single Day Surgery Center is an extension of the physician's office. As such, there is great continuity of care in a private, personal atmosphere that gives patient, family, and physician more control over the surgery and recovery processes.

The friendly, reassuring atmosphere at TSDS begins in the intimate lobby, complete with a separate children's area full of playthings to comfort and keep small children occupied as they wait for their own procedures or wait with other family members. The close proximity and immediate access families and patients have to one another are big benefits at Tallahassee Single Day Surgery. Family members are with the patient as much as possible, creating the best support system for rapid recovery and a relaxed approach prior to surgery.

The friendliness and personal touches complement the four state-of-the-art operating rooms and licensed 12-bed recovery room. A drawing lab, licensed pharmacy, and x-ray area allow the staff of 47 to serve some 4,000 patients a year efficiently and effectively. Tallahassee Single Day Surgery Center is owned by 38 surgeons, and many others in the Tallahassee area have privileges and use the facility for their outpatient procedures. Physicians schedule operations in a wide range of areas at TSDS, from general surgery, dentistry/oral surgery, and gynecology to otolaryngology, opthalmology, and orthopedics to plastic/reconstructive surgery, podiatry, and urology. Having TSDS available reduces the cost of these procedures by 30 to 60 percent, provides the patient and family with a more positive surgical experience, gives the physician greater control, and the general community a buffer from rising medical costs.

Especially in light of reforms in health care, Tallahassee Single Day Surgery Center is on the leading edge of the trend towards less invasive and more outpatient-oriented procedures. To stay there, the company follows the principles of continuous quality improvement, a philosophy that is promoted throughout TSDS, from using patient and customer feedback to continuous training for employees. This approach guarantees success in achieving the mission of Tallahassee Single Day Surgery, which is to provide high quality outpatient elective surgical care to the people of Leon County and surrounding referral areas in Florida and neighboring states. This is done as cost effectively as possible in an independent,

TALLAHASSEE SINGLE DAY SURGERY CENTER

pleasant, and convenient workplace for physicians, and within the financial range of patients' capabilities.

Accredited by the Joint Commission on Accreditation of Healthcare Organizations, Tallahassee Single Day Surgery has been recognized by that organization for its innovative surgical care. Additional recognition has come from being an involved member of the community; TSDS sponsors "PhoneFriend," an after school telephone support line for children, and has helped with drug-free rallies, the community health care annual fund-raisers, and has donated medication and equipment to the Saint Petersburg, Russia, Children's Hospital. In 1994 the Tallahassee Chamber of Commerce gave TSDS a second runner-up award in its Business of Excellence Award in the area of community service and innovation, and the Junior League of Tallahassee named TSDS a "Friend of the League" for the "Phone-Friend" program.

Tallahassee Single Day Surgery Center is on the leading edge of the trend towards less invasive and more outpatient-oriented procedures.

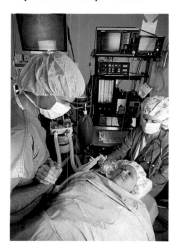

Through its dedication to service both within its doors and out in the community, Tallahassee Single Day Surgery has become a valuable part of Tallahassee and will remain so far into the future. ◆

At Tallahassee Single Day Surgery Center there is great continuity of care in a private, personal atmosphere that gives patient, family, and physician more control over the surgery and recovery processes.

The MARKETPLACE

◆

Governor's Square presence in a city the size of Tallahassee is evidence that the once-sleepy southern city has grown into a modern, sophisticated marketplace. Photo by Robert M. Overton.

GOVERNOR'S
SQUARE

Located just one mile east of Florida's Capitol and Tallahassee's downtown, Governor's Square shopping center offers shoppers in a tri-state region the best and latest in retail products and services. Its presence in a city the size of Tallahassee is proof that the once-sleepy southern capital city is growing up into a modern, sophisticated urban center. From its sleek architecture to its unusual assortment of shops to its unique dedication to the environment, Governor's Square is a reflection of what Tallahassee has become and a harbinger of what the city will be.

The shopping center opened in 1979 with three leading department stores and 228,000 square feet of gross leasable space. Along with the anchors J.C. Penney, Sears, and Maas Brothers (now Burdines), there were several locally owned, independent stores—James Surrey, Ltd., Vanity Shoes, The Frame Up, Garnet & Gold, and Top Stop, among others.

The Governor's Square management team, Eric Litz and Luanne Lenberg, have been with the shopping center for nearly a decade, providing steady, secure oversight and developing long-term, lasting partnerships with the merchants and the regional community.

Throughout its history, Governor's Square has enjoyed a longer-than-industry-average lease life for its stores, and a comparatively high proportion of locally owned and operated stores. These facts, along with the shopping center's record of having an increase in gross sales volume every year since it opened, reflect the healthy, profitable, and mutually beneficial relationship between the center merchants, the center management, and Governor's Square customers.

Governor's Square was developed and is managed by an affiliate of The Rouse Company, one of the largest publicly held real estate development companies in the country. Headquartered in Columbia, Maryland, The Rouse Company operates more than 200 properties encompassing office, retail, research and development, industrial, and hotel space, with an asset value in the early 1990s of $4.5 billion. Properties are located in 26 states, the District of Columbia, and Canada. Rouse is the renowned developer of the city of Columbia, Maryland, as well.

Among its properties are 78 retail centers, of which Governor's Square is one. These centers have more than 47 million square feet of space, including 26 million square feet occupied by 149 department stores. The remaining 21 million square feet are leased to approximately 8,000 small merchants, who had total sales of $4.7 billion in 1992. The Governor's Square management team is led by Eric Litz, vice president and general manager, and Luanne Lenberg, manger, sales and marketing. Both Eric and Luanne hold credentials from the ICSC in their respective fields. This team has been with the shopping center for nearly a decade, providing steady, secure oversight and developing long-term, lasting partnerships with the merchants and the regional community.

Governor's Square is situated on a 103-acre site, surrounded by over 7 million square feet of office space within a two-mile radius, much of which is dedicated to state government offices. This location gives the mall a more urban character than might be expected in a city the size of Tallahassee, and this "flavor" is undoubtedly part of its success. The shopping center is also centrally located for the 50,000 college students attending Florida State University, Florida Agricultural and Mechanical University, and Tallahassee Community College. Approximately 8 million visitors per year come to Governor's Square, easily accessible from Interstate 10, U.S. 90, and Highway 27.

By the early '90s, the success of Governor's Square catalyzed a major expansion and renovation program. The Phase II expansion plan increased the center's size to over 1 million square feet, giving it super regional drawing power with over 140 shops, three restaurants, a pushcart market place, and four major department stores. The 1993 expansion added 30,000 square feet to Burdines, a new two-story, 120,000-foot specialty retail wing, and a fourth department store, Dillard's, with 200,000 square feet on two levels and enclosed parking for 200 vehicles.

The unique blend of local and national stores provides unusually sophisticated product availability to Tallahasseeans, residents of the tri-state market area, and visitors passing

through. The original local shops, many of which are in their second decade of business at Governor's Square, are delighted with the turn the shopping center has taken. They see the arrival of such well-known names as Dillard's, GapKids, Eddie Bauer, The Bombay Company, The Disney Store, Gymboree, The Body Shop, and Wet Seal as magnets that attract customers and keep the competitive spirit alive.

Another unique feature for a shopping center of its size in a city the size of Tallahassee is Governor's Square's three sit-down restaurants—Morrison's Cafeteria, Ruby Tuesday's, and Mozzarella's—and the 12-spot food court, with over 500 seats. These establishments not only serve shoppers, but they also draw in visitors and are popular among Tallahassee's "dining out" crowd. Equally appealing are the specialty market pushcarts positioned throughout the center, a Rouse Company trademark, which were first developed at Faneuil Hall Marketplace in Boston.

Another signature feature of Governor's Square is its heavy emphasis on customer service. Customers are treated as if they were guests, and Governor's Square has instituted several unique approaches to assuring that each customer's visit is as pleasant and relaxing as possible. For those who shop with small children, there are strollers of every size and description available, free of charge. Wheelchairs and motorized shopping vehicles allow shoppers to move freely about the two-story, three-wing facility.

A permanent customer service center, located on the upper level Sears wing, provides visitors with a postal area, copying service, telephone facility for people with hearing impairments (TDD), and all kinds of local and regional information. Providing relocation data, Tallahassee Area Convention and Visitors Bureau brochures, and Chamber of Commerce literature, the customer service center functions as an excellent way for strangers to get to know Tallahassee.

Throughout the shopping center, customer service kiosks are staffed by friendly, helpful employees who assist shoppers with all kinds of questions. One of the most popular services is the product database. A customer can ask if a certain product is available in the mall, and the customer service associate can call it up on the computer and locate it in the appropriate store(s).

Governor's Square's commitment to its customers and guests continues outside the building, with ample parking, good lighting, 24-hour security patrols, and beautiful landscaping. In fact, the facility has received three awards related to its environmental sensitivity. In 1985 the shopping center received the Leon County Environmental Award for its original development. For Phase II, Governor's Square was recognized by the City of Tallahassee Growth Management Department for its cooperation in furthering the protection of the city's environment. Also in recognition of the Phase II development process, the Leon County Commission awarded Governor's Square its second Leon County Environmental Award in recognition of the regional storm water management system installed in conjunction with the project.

As a member of the community, Governor's Square has been a generous sponsor of numerous charitable events, raising more than $400,000 toward community projects, and donating the proceeds from its beautiful center court fountain to area agencies that serve children and families.

The commitment to Tallahassee is apparent in many ways at Governor's Square, from the partnerships established with the merchants, especially the locally owned and operated ones, to attention to the environment in a city where this matters very much, to its corporate citizenship. Because of its exciting, cutting edge approach to retail and the fascinating, appealing mix of national, regional, and local stores, coupled with good restaurants and food choices, and its commitment to Tallahassee, Governor's Square has become the dominant shopping center in the region and will continue its commitment to remain so into the next century. ◆

The arrival of such well-known company names attracts customers and keep the competitive spirit alive.

Few hotels in Tallahassee are owned and operated by national companies, but when CapStar Hotels was expanding its markets in 1989, Florida's capital city looked promising, and the Ramada Inn North was purchased. Among the nation's top 15 independent hotel management firms and headquartered in Washington, D.C., CapStar has since acquired a second property in Tallahassee, Ramada Inn Capitol View, reaffirming the original prediction of steady growth and a desirable market.

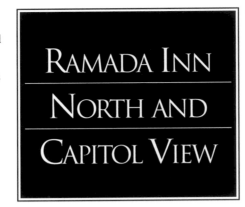

RAMADA INN
NORTH AND
CAPITOL VIEW

of attention to detail. This is evident in the hotel's $1.4 million renovation, invested primarily in guest room comforts and upgrades, including furnishings and the amenities that business travelers appreciate. The hotel serves travelers who visit Tallahassee only briefly, vacationers, airline crews, and government workers. Corporate business travel represents a large part of the facility's growth in trade in recent years, and contributed to CapStar's decision to acquire another property in Tallahassee.

Tallahassee has several hotel seasons—spring, when the legislature is in session; summer, when state, regional, and national sporting events come to the area; and fall, when Florida State

The Ramada Inn Capitol View's 145 guest rooms and four suites support the largest amount of meeting space available on Apalachee Parkway, the east-west artery that leads directly to the Capitol.

University and Florida Agricultural and Mechanical University boast two of the nation's finest football teams and bands. Throughout the year state government and business travelers demand lodging, and the Ramada properties are prepared to meet the needs of all of these visitors.

The Ramada Inn North is conveniently located just off the Interstate 10 intersection with North Monroe Street, a major north-south artery. This particular intersection has the largest number of hotel rooms along Interstate 10 between Jacksonville, Florida, and San Diego, California, making it an ideal stopover for travelers. It is an especially ideal stop for tourists from the west on their way to and from Orlando, as the travel time to that destination is an easy five hours from the Interstate 10/North Monroe interchange. Among the hotels located here, the Ramada Inn North enjoys one of the highest ratings and highest occupancy rates.

The Ramada Inn Capitol View is just that, located within sight of Tallahassee's Capitol and legislative buildings, a quick five-minute trip to the heart of state government and downtown. Purchased and given a $1.3 million remodeling in 1994, the Capitol View property is located on approximately four acres. Its 145 guest rooms and four suites support the largest amount of meeting space available on Apalachee Parkway, the east-west artery that leads directly to the Capitol. Its restaurant, Star's Cafe and Bar, features starry decorative motifs, American cuisine, and photos of local, state, and national sports and theatrical celebrities.

The North property, located on 12 acres and consisting of three buildings and a main tower, is popular in large part because

The North property has the area's largest single-room ballroom without columns, and 11 meeting and banquet rooms. With 198 guest rooms, 7 of which are suites, the Ramada Inn North is the area's largest single-facility conference and convention host.

But the Ramada Inn North is very popular with Tallahassee area residents, too. Weddings, sorority and fraternity parties, retirement and sports banquets, and family reunions are just a few of the events fully supported by the North's full-service catering and banquet capabilities. Housing the area's first and longest-running comedy club, the Comedy Zone, the Ramada Inn North has consistently attracted leading national and regional talent to perform in front of packed houses. The hotel's nightclub, Dooley's Downunder, has its own following. Decorated in an Australian theme, the club features some of the country's top jazz talents. Wynton Marsalis has played Dooley's, as have Herb Harris, Travis Shook, and Marcus Roberts. In fact, Roberts, a Tallahassee resident, uses Dooley's Downunder as a live practice arena for his latest compositions and arrangements before taking them into the studio for recording or onto the road for concert performances.

Star's Cafe and Bar, the Ramada Inn Capitol View's restaurant, features starry decorative motifs, American cuisine, and photos of local, state, and national celebrities.

A delight to Tallahasseeans and visitors alike is the hotel's restaurant, the Monroe Street Grille. Located off the tower's lushly decorated lobby, the Grille serves three meals a day as if it were a big city restaurant, according to the *Tallahassee Democrat's* food critic, Ashby Stiff. In 1990 and again in 1994, he gave the Grille an impressive four out of five "hats" for excellence in cuisine, environment, and service. It is rare for Mr. Stiff to be so gracious in two consecutive visits, no matter how infrequently they are made, so the Grille is justifiably proud of its impact on the area's leading dining connoisseur. In 1994 a 100-gallon lobster tank was added to the Grille, featuring live Maine lobsters flown in weekly. The Grille also serves one of the area's largest Sunday brunch buffets and provides one of Tallahassee's largest soup and salad bars, two more drawing cards for the nontraveling public.

Both hotels offer complimentary shuttle service to the Tallahassee Regional Airport, and the North property has a fitness center arrangement with a local health club that is completely full-service, and available 19 hours a day.

The extent of the services and amenities offered at both Ramada properties is unusual in Tallahassee, but the market justifies it, according to Will Gibbs, vice president of operations for CapStar Hotels and on-site manager of the North property. "Since 1989 we have found the Tallahassee market most receptive to a national company coming in to the hotel industry. As compared to other markets around the country that we are involved with, we find Tallahassee to be an unusually stable market, primarily driven off the growth of state government and the universities."

To prove their commitment to the Tallahassee area as a community, the Ramada properties have representation on the Leon County Tourist Development Council, the Tallahassee Area Convention and Visitors Bureau, and the Tallahassee Area Chamber of Commerce. Says Gibbs, "We are very excited about corporate growth that the Tallahassee Chamber has helped acquire. And we are glad to see the community's concern for growth management, too, so that Tallahassee remains an attractive place to live." Together the two properties employ approximately 250 people, making CapStar one of the area's largest employers.

To maintain its excellent standing in the community and premier services to its guests and diners, both Ramada properties are involved with the Florida State University School of Hospitality, one of the eight top schools in the nation. Students take tours through the properties, come to work as interns, and

The Ramada Inn North is conveniently located just off the Interstate 10 intersection with North Monroe Street, a major north-south artery. Among the hotels located in this area, the Ramada Inn North enjoys one of the highest ratings and highest occupancy rates.

often stay on with CapStar and are promoted throughout the company. The school uses the North property, especially, as a training facility and classroom, exposing the students to state-of-the-art computer and telephone systems, preparing them for jobs in larger, more metropolitan markets.

The goal of the two Ramada Inns in Tallahassee is to exceed their customers' expectations by anticipating their needs. Proof of their ability to do so is in the North property's 1993 receipt of CapStar's Exceeding Expectations Award, the company's highest honor, given annually to the single property that demonstrates the best in overall operations excellence. There is no doubt that Ramada Inns North and Capitol View will continue to be bright spots in Tallahassee's hotel and restaurant industries for years to come. ◆

The very nature of the design—a lovely courtyard replete with gazebo, lush plantings, and lots of shade—makes Courtyard by Marriott an ideal lodging facility in a city known for its Southern heritage and remarkable trees.

Many travelers agree, for the Courtyard enjoys one of the highest occupancy rates in Tallahassee. The target market includes those who travel to the capital regularly and occasionally, visitors to corporate offices, and, increasingly, weekend tourists. Tallahassee's move to become a major sports event host means high demand for weekend rooms beyond the popular football and basketball seasons. Although its primary niche is the business traveler, the Courtyard is as equally committed to providing a comfortable and user-friendly environment for pleasure travelers. Even so, the hugely dominant market in Tallahassee is legislators, lobbyists, and legislative session visitors, who create a true "boom" season during the spring.

Although it has expanded its market to include pleasure travelers, the Courtyard remains committed to its primary niche, the business traveler. Each of the 154 rooms has a separate seating area for working or relaxing, a desk, a computer jack for laptop use, in-room movies, and voice mail. For people planning longer stays, there are 14 suites. Each suite boasts a refrigerator, bar, and microwave oven, perfect amenities to create a "home-away-from-home" atmosphere. The Courtyard continually upgrades and adds to in-room amenities to make each individual's stay as productive, yet relaxing, as possible.

The common areas of the hotel include a comfortable lobby, spacious lounge, restaurant, and conference rooms. To help unwind at the end of the day, there is an exercise room with

COURTYARD BY
MARRIOTT

the latest fitness machines, a whirlpool for unknotting tired muscles, and the beautiful pool and courtyard.

But hotels must deal with the permanent residents of their locations as well as the transient customers. So the Courtyard by Marriott strives to be a good corporate citizen by participating in a variety of activities. The 60 employees contribute annually to the United Way, and the managers are guest speakers to classes in Florida State University's nationally renowned hospitality program. The Courtyard sponsors a regular internship with Florida A & M University to increase upper-level management opportunities for minorities and relies on the area's college students to staff its full- and part-time positions.

Tallahassee's business community revolves around relationships, and the Courtyard invests plenty of time and talent in fostering cooperative corporate relations. The facility has hosted the Tallahassee Chamber of Commerce's popular Business After Hours, a monthly social hour for Chamber members. The semi-tropical courtyard has been the setting for a lively and exotic Caribbean festival party, numerous weddings, and receptions.

To stay on the cutting edge of critical hospitality issues, the Courtyard is heavily involved in the Hotel/Motel Association,

Although it has expanded its market to include pleasure travelers, the Courtyard remains committed to its primary niche, the business traveler.

the Tallahassee Area Convention and Visitors Bureau, and the Tourist Development Council. Through these organizations, the Courtyard by Marriott contributes to resolving issues of concern to the lodging and general community, such as guest safety, and helps to secure the rights for special events to attract additional visitors to Tallahassee.

Through all this hard work, what guests experience is a pleasant stay in a very nice hotel in a lovely city. Each room at the Courtyard is made to order for people seeking comfortable, quality lodging at a mid-range rate—just what you'd expect in a hotel "designed by business travelers for business travelers" that also understands the weekend vacationer. ◆

The very nature of the design—a lovely courtyard replete with gazebo, lush plantings, and lots of shade—makes Courtyard by Marriott an ideal lodging facility in a city known for its Southern heritage.

The Tallahassee Area Convention and Visitors Bureau motto—visitors make "cents"—is evident by the more than 2 million visitors who travel to the Tallahassee area each year, spending $242 million, generating $2.5 million in local sales tax, and supporting 6,200 jobs.

A not-for-profit hospitality industry association, the Convention and Visitors Bureau works with local businesses to "sell" the Tallahassee area as a visitor destination and provide visitor services. Convention and Visitors Bureau members, representing businesses from attractions, hotels, and restaurants to printers and florists, share a commitment to support local economic development through the visitor industry.

Complemented by targeted advertising and public relations, Convention and Visitors Bureau programs focus on promoting Tallahassee to groups including meeting/conventions, sporting events, motorcoach tours, and motion picture and television production.

Promoting meeting/convention services equal to those of larger cities and blended with small town charm, the Convention and Visitors Bureau targets specialty small- to medium-size social, educational, religious, and fraternal groups in addition to the more traditional association, government, and corporate meetings. Recent meeting/convention accomplishments include the American Pharmaceutical Association, Kenneth Copeland Ministries, the Goldwing Road Riders, and the Florida Council for the Social Studies.

Well-publicized Convention and Visitors Bureau sports marketing successes include the Florida Law Enforcement Games, generating 8,000 visitors and $3 million; the Sunshine State Games, resulting in 10,000 visitors and $4 million; and designation as the three-year training site for the 1996 British Olympic Team, the second largest delegation in the world. The Convention and Visitors Bureau sports marketing program is supported by the 51-member volunteer Tallahassee Sports Council.

The Convention and Visitors Bureau also promotes Tallahassee as a group leisure travel destination in the motorcoach (bus) tour and international markets. Tallahassee is an established stop-over destination for groups like St. Tours, averaging 400 one-night stops through Tallahassee each year. Convention and Visitors Bureau efforts are now directed toward developing destination tours like Springtacular, a two- to five-night tour package promoting area attractions and entertainment culminating with the Springtime Tallahassee festival.

TALLAHASSEE AREA CONVENTION AND VISITORS BUREAU

The Convention and Visitors Bureau also operates the Tallahassee Office of Film and Television, responding to production inquiries and promoting the area as a location for photo shoots, commercials, and motion picture filming. Credits range from a Lands' End catalog shoot to filming for the background scenes of a Universal Studios movie starring Patrick Swayze and Wesley Snipes.

Comprehensive, quality visitor and group services, provided through the Tallahassee Area Visitor Information Center located in the New Capitol Building, further complement Convention and Visitors Bureau objectives. Services include a toll-free visitor information hotline, suggested itineraries, walking and driving tours, and visitor brochures like the "Visitor's Guide" and "Tallahassee Events" calendar.

Launched by the Chamber of Commerce, the Convention and Visitors Bureau was incorporated in 1986 in response to the community's need for a dedicated visitor marketing and service organization. Through the combined efforts of the local visitor

Located on the West Plaza Level of the New Capitol Building, the Tallahassee Area Visitor Information Center greets Tallahassee area visitors with Southern-style hospitality.

industry and business community, Leon County's first two-percent lodging tax was passed in 1988, setting the Convention and Visitors Bureau on an aggressive, independent course of success.

Today, the Convention and Visitors Bureau is funded primarily by Local Option Tourist Development Tax revenues appropriated through a public-private sector partnership through the Leon County Tourist Development Council with the board of county commissioners. Membership dues provide the next largest portion of annual revenues. A volunteer board of directors sets the direction and monitors the progress of all Convention and Visitors Bureau programs.

Best known as Florida's capital city, Tallahassee is often described as the "other Florida" with its deep-rooted history, rolling hills, and Southern-style hospitality. From its country canopied roads, capitol buildings, and plantation homes to its natural attractions, outdoor adventures, and special events, Tallahassee is a Florida even few residents have really seen. It is Florida with a Southern accent. ◆

BIBLIOGRAPHY

Ausley, Allison. *More Than A Bank: The History of the Capital City Bank Group, The First 100 Years.* Tallahassee, Florida: Capital City Bank Group, 1993.

Balfour, Robert C. Jr. *This Land I Have Loved.* Tallahassee, Florida: Rose Printing Co., 1975.

Bettinger, Julie S. "15 Years of Tallahassee: A Celebration," *Tallahassee Magazine,* March/April, 1994: 18.

——————. "Looking Back, The Floridan Hotel: The Other Capitol," *Tallahassee Magazine,* July/August, 1993: 74.

Cotterell, Bill. "Leon County/Tallahassee, Tree Hugging and Tassel Loafers." In *Almanac of Florida Politics,* by Tom Fielder, author; Margaret Kempel, editor. Miami, Florida: The *Miami Herald,* 1994.

Dunn, Hampton. *Yesterday's Tallahassee.* Miami, Florida: E. A. Seemann Publishing, Inc., 1974.

Ellis, Mary Louise and William Warren Rogers. *Tallahassee: Favored Land: A History of Tallahassee and Leon County.* Norfolk, Virginia Beach, Virginia: The Donning Company, 1988.

——————. *Tallahassee and Leon County: A History and Bibliography.* Tallahassee, Florida: Florida Department of State, 1986.

Fisher, Barbara Gene. *Meridian Markers.* Great Neck, New York: Todd and Honeywell, 1984.

Florida State University. "The State of Your Future." Tallahassee, Florida: Florida State University, 1994.

Groene, Bertram H. *Ante-Bellum Tallahassee.* Tallahassee, Florida: The Florida Heritage Foundation, 1971.

Haase, Ronald W. *Classic Cracker, Florida's Wood-Frame Vernacular Architecture.* Sarasota, Florida: Pineapple Press, Inc., 1992.

Hayden, Clara R. *A Century of Tallahassee Girls: As Viewed From the Leaves of Their Diaries.* Atlanta: Foote & Davies Co., n.d.

Jahoda, Gloria. *The Other Florida.* New York: Charles Scribner's Sons, 1967.

Johnson, Malcolm B. *I Declare! A Collection of Editorial Commentaries.* Comp. by Ray Reynolds. Tallahasee, Florida: *The Tallahassee Democrat,* 1983.

The Junior League of Tallahassee. *Thymes Remembered.* Tallahassee, Florida: Junior League of Tallahassee, Inc., n.d.

Ketchum, Eleanor. *Tales of Tallahassee.* Tallahassee, Florida: Jerry Dye and Associates, Inc., 1976.

Mickler, Delia Appleyard and Carolyde Phillips O'Bryan. *Colonel's Inn Caterers: Tallahassee Historical Cookbook.* Tallahassee, Florida: Rose Printing Company, 1984.

Morris, Joan Perry and Martee Wills. *Seminole History.* Jacksonville, Florida: South Star Publishing Company, 1987.

Paisley, Clifton. *From Cotton to Quail—An Agricultural Chronicle of Leon County, Florida, 1860-1967.* Gainesville, Florida: University of Florida Press, 1968.

Smith, Hale G., PhD. *Tallahassee: Historic Scenic Capital of Florida.* Tallahassee, Florida: Talla., Inc., 1955.

The Tallahassee Junior Woman's Club. *Canopy Roads Collected Recipes.* Tallahassee, Florida: Tallahassee Junior Woman's Club, 1979.

Tallahassee—The Capital City of Florida. Jacksonville, Florida: Arnold Printing Company, n.d.

TALLAHASSEE ENTERPRISES

INDEX

This book was set in Trajan, Times Roman, and Times Bold Italic
at Community Communications, Inc., Montgomery, Alabama,
and printed on 80 lb. Warren Flo Text.